T0196920

You'll Laugh a Little, You'll Cry a Little

BRANDON BOSWELL

YOU'LL LAUGH A LITTLE, YOU'LL CRY A LITTLE

iUniverse books may be ordered through booksellers or by contacting:

iUniverse
1663 Liberty Drive
Bloomington, IN 47403
www.iuniverse.com
1-800-Authors (1-800-288-4677)

ISBN: 978-1-5320-8769-1 (sc)
ISBN: 978-1-5320-8768-4 (e)

Library of Congress Control Number: 2019920558

Print information available on the last page.

iUniverse rev. date: 12/17/2019

For Ashley & Shelley, Dana, and Steph

For Trish and Cindy:
Demos Always and Forever!

For my family: Thank you for your
love and encouragement.

Most importantly, For the loving God who
put all these wonderful people in my life.

WASHING YOUR HANDS CAN BE HAZARDOUS TO YOUR HEALTH

(INTRODUCTION)

The words you are about to read are ones I never thought would be written in a book I never thought would exist. Five years ago when I published what I thought would be my final book, I remember thinking, *Well, this is it. It's over. I will never write another book. I have NO more books left in me to write!* Apparently, God must not have gotten that memo.

Several months ago, I was just doing my own thing when it happened. I heard the voice of God. God spoke to me! He didn't speak to me out loud, though. I'm a Baptist, and we consider that a felony. God did, however, speak to my heart. He said, "Brandon, guess what? You know how you thought you had NO more books left in you to write? Well, you were wrong! You just needed to wait awhile for something new to write about, and now it's finally time to get started on a new book! Aren't you excited?"

My response was, "Not really, Lord, I'm not."

The Lord's response to my response was, "Well, too bad, 'cause it's going to happen anyway."

When people find out I have written books, they ask me a lot of questions. Some questions are easy to answer like, "How long does it take you to write a book?" The answer: Way too long. Another question I get asked is, "Do you enjoy writing?" My response is that I do enjoy writing … when I'm not actually doing any writing. Once I start writing, however, it's a whole other story. Once writer's block kicks in, it seems like the "whole other story" will never see the light of day.

Another question I often get asked is, "How do you come up with material to write about?" That's actually more painful than writer's block. To come up with material, I actually have to leave my house, which I find to be so inconvenient.

I'm a homebody. I like being a homebody. When I'm not at work or church, you will almost always find me in my house. From time to time, though, I have friends who will want to get together to make sure I'm still alive and they want to do this in locations that are *not* my house. This means I have to, ugh, LEAVE my house and go out in public. Double ugh!

I like people, but I don't like crowds. The problem is, though, when you get a bunch of people together in the same place and more keep coming, before you know it, a crowd has formed. I'll put this in mathematical terms:

People + More People = Way Too Many People (Crowds).

When you have friends who you love, though, you learn to make sacrifices, which isn't that bad except for the part where you have to do things that you don't want to do.

* * *

Not long ago, my friend Sheila suggested we eat at a little seafood restaurant in a nearby beachfront town, which I reluctantly agreed to. Don't get me wrong. I love Sheila and enjoy spending time with her, but I knew going on this trip would mean having to make some of those dreaded sacrifices I hate making. This would include:

Sacrifice One: Leaving my house. Self explanatory.

Sacrifice Two: Traveling. I hate riding in a vehicle for any extended period of time primarily because if my body parts were pieces of fruit, my bladder would be a grape and my prostate would be a cantaloupe that feels more like a watermelon. If I get nervous for any reason, I feel like I constantly have to use the bathroom. Trips to restaurants always make me nervous because I know as soon as I get there, I'll have to deal with (yep, you guessed it) Sacrifice Three: CROWDS.

On the day of our trip, Sheila picked me up promptly at 1:00 in the afternoon. I had wanted to do a later lunch in the hopes I could outsmart the crowds and show up when there weren't enough people there to "crowd" me.

The trip to the restaurant was uneventful. Sheila talked most of the way there. I listened. Since she actually has a life outside of her house, she likes to share it with me. When the day comes and I get a life, I'll return the favor and see how she likes it.

Forty minutes later, we arrived at the restaurant. We walked in, and of course, what did we see? A crowd! Plus, since we were in a waterfront town, we saw the worst kind of crowd: a tourist crowd. Tourist crowds have three goals in life: 1.) To eat, 2.) To shop, and 3.) To annoy those around them by whatever means necessary.

I would not be deterred, however. I was determined to have a nice lunch with Sheila. We soon found a table that wasn't completely surrounded by the tourist crowd. Moments later, the waitress came and we ordered our beverages and meals. I ordered the lemonade. Oh, how I wish I hadn't ordered the lemonade. It tasted so good, but as I kept sipping it over the course of the meal, I knew that before leaving the restaurant I would have to make Sacrifice Four: using a public restroom. When health inspectors visit restaurants, I don't know how much time they spend in the restroom, but whatever amount it is, it's not enough.

Lunch went well. Sheila and I talked about this and that. By the way, why is it whenever you get together with friends and talk about your lives, their "this" always seems so much better than your "that"?

About an hour or so later, we were finishing up our meal. Soon, it would be time for our waitress to return with the check, or in our case, checks, since Shelia and I usually go Dutch. Paying for our own meals just seems to work for us. Sheila has always seemed pretty insistent on it. I wonder if it's because she knows I work in an hourly wage job where I don't make a whole lot of money and she feels sorry for me and doesn't feel it's right to ask me to pay for her meal as well. If this is true, my goal is to somehow make her feel even sorrier for me so she will offer to pay for my meal, too.

By the time the meal was over, I had consumed two large glasses of lemonade. I knew Sheila would want to do some shopping after lunch, so I knew the time had now come to use the dreaded public restroom I had been fearing.

I excused myself and walked into the restroom. Little did I know things were about to take a turn for the worse. Within a couple of seconds of walking into the restroom, I could tell something wasn't right. I felt like I was about to lose my balance and fall flat on my face and butt simultaneously. I quickly discovered the floor was covered with some type of sticky, slippery substance. Perhaps someone had recently waxed the floor and hadn't cleaned up properly afterwards, who knows. The situation was made worse by the fact I was wearing a new pair of tennis shoes I hadn't really broken in yet.

Whenever I use a public restroom, I always wash my hands first. The trip from the door to the bathroom sink was one of the most harrowing experiences of my life. I almost lost my balance and fell multiple times, but I was determined to wash my hands. I'm a germ freak, and by not washing my hands the germs win and I lose. I was going to wash my hands even if it killed me. When I leave this world, I'm leaving it with a clean conscience and even cleaner hands.

I made it to the sink without falling and washed my hands. I *earned* that privilege. Next, I had to find the nearest toilet that appeared to be clean. Walking from the sink to the stalls wasn't any easier. It was almost like that restroom floor was alive and out to get me. With every step I had to maintain my balance. I knew I could only do this for so long, so I made Sacrifice Five: giving up finding a clean toilet and settling for a clean-ish toilet.

Seconds later, I finally found one that met my basic criteria. Of course, the floor on the inside of the stall was just as slippery as it was on the outside. I walked in and attempted to close the stall door with my back while I propped myself against it. When I use a public restroom, my goal is to touch as little as I have to while in there. On this day, I had a new goal, however, and that was to not lose my balance and fall face first into the clean-ish toilet.

The entire time I was in the stall, I could feel my feet slipping. I found myself giving myself a pep talk. I told my feet, "You will do your job and keep me from falling!" Unfortunately, at the same time, my bladder decided it didn't feel like working, and I now had to do whatever it took to remain upright long enough for my bladder to stop phoning it in and become a team player.

So, now I'm giving BOTH my feet and bladder simultaneous pep talks. Looking back, I probably should not have done this out loud. I don't even want to know what the people in the stalls next to me were thinking, but since this is a family-friendly book, we're not going to speculate.

Finally, it was "all systems go," and soon I was back outside the stall, ready to make one final trip to the sink to wash my hands before leaving. The floor hadn't gotten any less slippery, however, so at the last second, I decided not to take any more steps than necessary. Slowly, I reversed course and carefully made my way to the door. It is for reasons such as this why I always carry my trusty bottle of hand sanitizer as a backup, making it one of the best blessings God has ever bestowed on mankind.

After making it safely outside of the restroom without sustaining any injuries, I breathed a sigh of relief. Before we left, I informed our waitress about the restroom floor and asked her to please let someone know how slippery it was. If anyone fell they could be injured. There could even be a lawsuit. Of course, the more I thought about a lawsuit, I was like, *Maybe I should go back and wash my hands after all. It REALLY does pay to be clean.*

Sheila and I left the restaurant and walked around the shopping complex surrounding the restaurant and browsed a couple of shops. Of course, soon I had to use the bathroom yet again. My bladder may get off to a slow start, but once it gets to work, it doesn't stop until the job is done.

Thankfully, we found a little movie theater nearby a few doors down from the restaurant. The staff was kind enough to let me use their restroom while Sheila waited in the lobby. It's funny because growing up, Sheila and I went to a conservative church school where we were warned to avoid movie theaters. The movies shown in them were considered sinful and potential gateways to Hell. I don't know about that, but the theater we were in had a nice clean men's room where I was able to roam about freely without slipping. Whether or not a movie theater is a gateway to Hell, I couldn't tell you. What I can tell you is that a clean men's room inside a movie theater is a little piece of Heaven.

* * *

Life is complicated. One moment you feel like you're on top of the world, and the next, you're performing the greatest balancing act of your life as you try to avoid landing face first in the toilet. That's life in a nutshell.

Good or bad, the events in our lives help shape us into who we are and what we will become. Writing this book proved to be both an exciting and emotional experience for me. As I sat at the computer writing the stories you are about to read, I often found myself laughing out loud, whereas other times I was trying to fight back the tears.

It's my hope that as you read this book, sometimes you'll laugh a little and perhaps even cry a little, too. It's also my hope you will remember that if you have family, friends, and most importantly, faith in God, you will know that no matter what life throws at you, you will never laugh or cry alone.

THANK YOU, MS. FRANCES

When I was about fifteen, I had an experience that, to this day, holds a special place in my heart. At the time, there was an older lady in my church we called Ms. Frances. Her husband, Rev. Aycock, was our Minister to Senior Adults. His job included heading up outreach ministries to the elderly members of our congregation and the surrounding community.

First, let me tell you about Rev. Aycock. He was one of the greatest preachers I ever knew. He knew the Bible backwards and forwards, and he lived it. This man loved God, loved people, and for those of us who remember him, he loved (L-O-V-E-D) to pray. Rev. Aycock prayed some of the most heartfelt prayers I have ever heard. He also prayed some of LONGEST prayers I ever heard. He was known by those of us who loved him as "the man of the never-ending prayer," or "Rev. Praycock," for short.

Let me tell you about Rev. Aycock's prayers. If, for example, someone in our church was having surgery that week, we knew Rev. Aycock would be lifting them up in prayer that Sunday if he was preaching. Not only would he pray for the person having surgery, it was also very likely he would be praying as well for the doctor performing the surgery, the nurses assisting the doctor during the surgery, the hospital administrator in charge to make sure there were enough operating rooms available to perform the surgery, the maintenance staff at the hospital that they would have the operating room properly cleaned in time for the surgery, the lady behind the counter at the hospital gift shop that she wouldn't run out of stuffed animals with shirts that read "I'm Bear-y Glad You're Still Alive" for after the surgery, and the folks who work in the hospital cafeteria that they wouldn't run out of chicken tenders because that was the favorite food of the person having the surgery, etc. etc. After about the fifteenth "etc." many of us in the congregation felt like we would need surgery, too. When Rev. Aycock said "Amen," we *all* said "Amen."

Let's get back to Ms. Frances. This story takes place on a Sunday evening. Our youth group had left the church to attend an event at another church just outside of town. By the time we returned to our church, the evening service was about halfway over. I usually attended the evening service and didn't like missing it, but I didn't want to walk in and disrupt the service. I chose to remain outside of the sanctuary.

As I was walking along the hallway outside of the sanctuary, I noticed the door to Rev. Aycock's office was open. I walked over to see Ms. Frances sitting alone on the small love seat on the side wall of the tiny room. I thought it was odd she would be in the office and not in the service. When I spoke to her, she told me that she started to have a coughing fit during the service. Since she didn't want to disrupt the service, she decided to step out. I decided to sit down on the chair next to her and keep her company for a few minutes. We ended up talking for about half an hour. There's a good chance Rev. Aycock was praying the entire time we were in there. After the service ended, Rev. Aycock came to check on Ms. Frances. I could tell he was glad someone had been there to keep her company.

The evening I spent talking with Ms. Frances has always been special to me. I can't remember anything we talked about, but it was still a nice memory. Being so young, I hadn't had as many experiences just sitting and talking to older adults. My grandparents were still alive back then and I loved being with them, but that felt different. When I talked to them, I always felt like I was just their little grandson, no matter how old I was. Even if I just zoned out and only pretended like I was listening, I knew I would still be compensated with my usual one dollar reward for just being in the room.

The experience I had with Ms. Frances was different. This was an older adult who I wasn't related to in any way. She could have asked me to leave her alone that evening, but she didn't. She took the time to talk to me, and I could tell she was genuinely interested in me and what I had to say. She didn't treat me like I was a little kid, but more like a young adult. That was a pretty awesome feeling. By the time I left church that night, I thought, *Wow, old people are pretty cool!* I only hope after talking to me, Ms. Frances thought, *Wow! Young people are pretty cool, too!*

It truly is the little things in life that matter. The simple act of checking on Ms. Frances that night turned into a cherished lifelong memory. What Ms. Frances taught me that evening about love and friendship in that tiny office was just as important as anything her husband could have taught me from behind the pulpit.

Sadly, Rev. and Mrs. Aycock are now both deceased, but I will never forget them or their impact on our church and my life. It's my sincere prayer that the younger people reading this will meet older adults like the Aycocks who will become a blessing to them. If you haven't met them yet, don't worry. Rev. Aycock taught me how to pray, and I promise I won't stop praying until you do.

GOD BLESS THE CHILDREN AND THOSE WHO HOLD THEM

Sometimes the sweetest moments come from the most unexpected events. This story takes place nearly fourteen years ago, and just like the story from the previous chapter, it also takes place in my church. Several months earlier, our long-time pastor had retired, and we now had an interim pastor. If you're not familiar with this term, an interim pastor is a pastor who fills in for a church after the previous pastor leaves and usually remains until a new pastor is hired. It's basically a substitute pastor.

If you're like me, when you think of substitutes, you think back to your schooldays when you had a substitute teacher while your regular teacher was out sick, had a family emergency, or was undergoing a psychiatric evaluation. On the substitute teacher's first day in class, you and your classmates felt morally obligated to take advantage of the situation by convincing the sub your regular teacher always finished class twenty minutes early and was required to buy ice cream sandwiches for the class every day. Did the sub believe you? Rarely, but you still felt you had to strike while the iron was hot.

Having an interim pastor in church is sort of like being back in school with a substitute teacher. In this case, though, the students are all grown up, and they're now on the board of deacons trying to convince the interim pastor their last pastor always finished the sermon at a quarter to noon and bought coffee and doughnuts for the congregation. It didn't work in school, and apparently it doesn't work in church, either.

At this time, my church had an interim pastor named Rev. Gurganus who had taken over after our last pastor retired after ten years of faithful service. It was hard seeing someone new standing behind the pulpit. I loved our former pastor.

On top of this, just prior to the arrival of Rev. Gurganus, the church had just gone through some major conflicts. Business meetings had felt like war zones. Long-time fellow church members felt like "the enemy within." People I had known in the church for years had turned on one another. People were screaming at one another. Accusations were being made. As one church member had said, it was like the Devil was sitting in the back row of the church just laughing his head off. The Devil knew all that was needed to destroy our church was to divide us into two warring factions. For a time, it proved to be successful.

In time and with God's help, peace was restored to the church, but the battle scars remained. A number of families left the church, never to return. They thought *we* were wrong. We thought *they* were wrong. Many of the people who were once our friends and spiritual mentors were now just painful memories.

Time passed, and Rev. Gurganus had now been our interim pastor for several months. While I found him to be a very nice older gentleman who preached a perfectly fine sermon, I still missed my former pastor. Plus, every Sunday I would look out and see row after row of empty pews where former long-time church members had once sat. Church didn't feel the same. I felt numb. My mindset was quickly becoming *Sing the songs, pass the plate, preach the sermon, pray the prayer, and leave.*

This story takes place one Sunday morning during a Parent/Child Dedication service. Usually, whenever we would hold this type of service, new parents were asked to come forward with their newborn children. The preacher would introduce the families, and the baby might be given a gift, such as a tiny Bible. Such services are very symbolic. The parents make a commitment before the church and God to raise their children up in a Godly home and teach them strong Christian values and morals throughout their young lives. I liked these types of services just fine, but having been single my whole life and not having children, these services had never meant much to me before. This dedication service, however, would prove to be very different.

The Parent/Child Dedication started out normal enough. The parents and their babies were asked to come to the front of the church. At this point, Rev. Gurganus introduced each family and child. After each baby was introduced, Rev. Gurganus did something I'll never forget. In previous dedication services, the pastor would just introduce the parents and their babies while the parents continued to hold them.

Rev. Gurganus had a slightly different approach. He was a grandfather and loved babies. He especially loved getting to hold babies, so that was exactly what he was going to do! After the first baby was introduced, Rev. Gurganus very carefully took the baby from the parent's arms and was soon cradling the baby in his own arms. The man was in seventh heaven.

In addition to holding each baby one at a time, Rev. Gurganus took full advantage of the situation and did something else I had never seen before but have never forgotten. With each baby he held, he carefully walked from the front of the church and walked up and down the aisles as he gently spoke to each one like they were his own grandchildren. He wanted the congregation to get a good look at those babies. I've seen some amazing acts of love before, but nothing has ever quite compared to the love I saw on display that Sunday morning. Church started to feel really good to me again after that Sunday.

If you were to ask me to give a dictionary definition of "love," I don't know if I could. On that Sunday morning, though, I could certainly give an example of love in action.

If we loved one another the same way Rev. Gurganus loved those babies, this world would be a much better place for children to grow up and for adults to grow old. Rev. Gurganus knew those babies were more than just the children of their parents. They were God's children, each one created with a special purpose and plan.

Young or old, weak or strong, rich or poor, born near or far away, we are all equal in God's eyes. When Jesus Christ died for our sins, He didn't die for a select few. He died for all. I've heard it said that when we have the urge to look down on others and choose to hate a select few, may we remember when Christ hung on the cross, looking down on those around Him, choosing to love all.

Thank you, Rev. Gurganus, for helping me to remember this.

Rest in peace.

GIANT TEETH HELP MAKE THE BEST SMILES

I have come to the conclusion this world would be a much better place if we had more giant teeth walking around it. That comment should make perfect sense to everyone, but for the handful of individuals who may be confused, allow me to explain.

Recently, I was running some errands with my parents around town. We were driving down a side street just off a busy boulevard. On one side of the street were the back entrances to several banks, and on the other side was a large dental office. Standing in front of the dental office stood a giant tooth, or rather, someone in a giant tooth costume decorated with black eyes and a big smile.

Presumably, this was someone the dental office had paid to dress up in costume to help promote their business. I guess there is always the chance it could have been some random crazy person who liked dressing up as a giant tooth who just wandered onto the front lawn of the dental office and when the office staff saw it, they were like, "Well, we should call the cops, but this is too good to pass up." More than likely, though, they were paid to be there. I hope they were paid. It was so hot that day I was afraid whoever was in that costume would pass out. By the way, if a giant tooth passes out from the heat, is it considered heat stroke or tooth decay?

I've never forgotten seeing that giant tooth on that warm, spring day. I sometimes wonder about the personal life of that tooth. I wonder if the tooth was single, or perhaps married with a couple of baby teeth at home. I also wonder if the tooth gets the respect it deserves, or do people give the tooth the brush off. And, is it actually more respectful to brush off a tooth than not to brush?

When people see a giant tooth standing on the side of the road, it's going to get a reaction. Some people might see the tooth and simply laugh it off. Others might look down on the tooth and say to themselves that never in a million years would they ever be willing to be a giant tooth for any reason. I looked at that giant tooth and one of the first things I thought was the following: Imagine if that giant tooth was standing there in front of the dental office, minding its own business, checking itself in the mirror to make sure it didn't have any plaque showing. All of a sudden, a bank alarm goes off from one of the banks across the street. Then, a lone bank robber runs out of the bank and the giant tooth decides to spring into action. The tooth chases down the robber, tackles and subdues him, and ties him up until the police arrive. What would a giant tooth have on them to tie up a bank robber? Maybe a large stash of dental floss, who knows? Then, for the icing on the cake, the next morning the front page of the local newspaper has the banner headline: *Giant Tooth Takes Bite Out of Crime.*

Beautiful, simply beautiful.

Okay, enough tooth puns. If I don't stop, I'm afraid I'll bite off more than I can chew. Sorry, I had to get that last one out of my system.

Why did I think that giant tooth was so cool? Simple. It was cool because it showed creativity in how that dental office advertised. That tooth made a lasting impression. I guess that's called a bite mark. Okay, okay, *now* I'll stop with the puns.

Seriously, though, that giant tooth reminded me that we need more creativity in this world. We get so caught up with all the struggles in our daily lives that we forget to take time to have a little fun along the way.

Working in retail like I do, it can feel like *everything* is about profit, profit, and more profit. Of course, if you don't make money you can't stay in business, but why can't we make money and show more creativity in how we do it?

For over a decade, I've worked for a member's only warehouse club. When I walk through the store, I take note of all the different items around me and the missed opportunities to be more creative and perhaps increase sales, too.

For example, from time to time, my store sells LEGO sets in the toy aisle. Usually someone will just stock the LEGO sets on the shelf, make sure the price sign is correct, and move on to the next item. Where is the fun in that?

I love LEGOs. I had a few LEGO sets as a kid, but as I grew up I lost interest and the pieces got lost or thrown away. I didn't rediscover the joys of building with LEGOs until a couple years ago. LEGOs are so much fun! When you buy a LEGO set, you can either build what the set is supposed to be by using the instructions, or you can throw out the instructions and build whatever you want. Being a man, I'm naturally inclined to disregard the instructions altogether.

When it comes to how my store sells LEGO products, I've always thought it would be great to build a large LEGO display on the sales floor so customers can see what you could build with just a little imagination. I would love to set up such a display. I've gotten really good at LEGO building, and I could create my own LEGO community for all to see. I could build cars, streets, and buildings completely out of LEGOs. What I really would love to build is a LEGO church. Give me enough pieces and I could build a LEGO megachurch. Heck, give me even more pieces and I could build a LEGO TV station on the campus of the megachurch so the LEGO preacher could have his own TV ministry. That LEGO preacher could become so successful I would have to build him his own LEGO private jet, and then he wouldn't have to ask for donations like other TV preachers do when they're trying to get their private jets. Think how cool a display like this could be! I say, "Let's get people's attention!"

Now, even though I work at a warehouse club, I actually work outside as an attendant at our on-site gas station. You might be saying, "Brandon, how could you show creativity while working at a gas station and increase business at the same time?"

Two words: free gas.

In theory, you could do this at most gas stations. You get the gas attendants in place at the pumps, the drivers come up, and you give them a few dollars in free gas (maybe from a gift card). The attendants could even pump the gas for them. The customers would go nuts! Can you imagine how many people would line up for free gas? Think of how many people may sign up for a store membership for the first time? It could be incredible! Incidentally, if any of the higher-ups from my company are reading this and want to put this idea into action, on whatever date you decide to do this, I'm afraid I'll either be on vacation or sick in bed or possibly dead. I haven't decided which one yet. Again I say, though, "Let's get people's attention!"

Companies should not be afraid to be more creative in how their employees interact with their customers. These same companies also need to show creativity in how they attract and keep qualified workers. No matter the size of the company, good work should always be rewarded. There are many ways to do this. For example, some companies use a star system to reward employees. If an employee earns enough gold stars, they win a reward. Say, if someone earns ten gold stars, they win lunch with their boss. If they earn fifteen gold stars, they win the right to *never* have lunch with their boss ever again.

Obviously, for any reward system to work, the right kind of rewards need to be offered. To be specific, rewards should be offered that employees actually, uh, want. This could include such things as gift cards, more days off, or, oh, what was that last one I wanted to mention? Oh, yeah … A PAY RAISE!! I know THAT would get my attention!

Another creative way to reward employees for their hard work is having an Employee of the Month award. I actually won this honor in my store for the month of July. I even had my picture taken and it was placed in a special Employee of the Month poster in our break room for all to see and ignore.

Since winning, however, changes were made company wide in Personnel, and at least in my own store, the Employee of the Month award doesn't seem to get much attention anymore. It used to be that every month we had a new Employee of the Month and they would get their picture on the poster in the break room. The next month would come and there would be a new Employee of the Month. The previous winner would have their picture removed and the newest winner would get their picture up in the break room.

While I've heard that my store still does Employee of the Month, as I'm writing this, my picture still remains on the same poster in the break room and has not been removed for over a year now. If the higher-ups at my company read this, it might be time to work harder at promoting Employee of the Month once more so other hard working employees can know the joy of winning. Until then, I'll just keep staring at my picture on the wall. I will admit it has done wonders for my self-esteem.

*   *   *

Retail businesses aren't the only organizations that need to show more creativity. I think churches also need to show more creativity in how they reach out to the communities they serve. Having been in the church my whole life, sometimes it feels like the unofficial motto of many churches is "We've Never Done It That Way Before and We Never Will!" (There's also another unofficial motto that "What Happens at the Liquor Store Stays at the Liquor Store," but I think that one only applies to Baptists.)

There are so many wonderful people in our churches, but it seems many times they are afraid to get out of their comfort zones for fear of what others may think. I say, "So what?"

For example, say you have someone who teaches a Sunday school class. Like any good Sunday school teacher, they will want to make the class more exciting so the students there will pay better attention and, at the same time, they can continue attracting new students, too. A little creativity can go a long way. Perhaps that Sunday school teacher could start dressing up as one of the Biblical characters from the lesson they are teaching that Sunday. That could really keep people's attention. Of course, that teacher would have to use some discretion. It might not be the best idea if they dressed up as say, Jezebel or Delilah. You wouldn't want the students walking out of class that week saying to one another, "Why did we *ever* ask that man to teach our class?"

Of course, a good church needs to have a good pastor. Pastors not only need to show creativity in how they serve their churches, but they also need to encourage their congregations to do the same. I've heard of some churches that occasionally have "theme" Sundays to boost attendance. I know of one church in my area that does something called "Round Up" Sunday where members of the congregation dress up like cowboys and cowgirls to make the service more fun, especially for the kids. Obviously, you don't want to lose sight of what church is about, but I think pastors shouldn't be afraid to wear a silly costume once in a while at the pulpit. The congregation might even enjoy the church service more. If a pastor isn't comfortable wearing a silly costume at first, that's fine. Start small. They could wear a silly watch so they know when to end the sermon on time. The congregation would *definitely* enjoy the church service more.

There are so many other wonderful ways to be creative in and through the church. For example, every summer my church holds its annual Vacation Bible School. I loved Vacation Bible School when I was a kid. My favorite part was snack time. For a few precious days, Kool-Aid and butter cookies with holes in the middle that you could put on your finger became part of a balanced diet.

One of the things I loved most about Vacation Bible School growing up was seeing all the great posters and artwork used to decorate our sanctuary where everyone came together before we would broke off into small groups. To this day, my church still decorates the sanctuary for Vacation Bible School with artwork that relates to whatever the theme is for that year. One year we had a sports theme, and the front of the sanctuary was decorated like a stadium. Another year was a jungle theme, and a family in the church had done artwork of large silhouettes of giraffes and elephants.

Years ago, I was asked to draw some of the artwork for Vacation Bible School. I was asked to draw a man climbing up a mountain. Every year we raised money for missions, and the man climbing up the mountain was going to be used to show how much money we were raising. The more money we raised, the higher the man climbing the mountain would go. While I'll admit I'm not a bad artist, I'm not the best at drawing people. When I finished, the man I drew looked as if he had fallen off that mountain a few times face first, but he was a trooper and kept getting back up. In any case, it was great using my love for drawing to help the church I love.

Another part of Vacation Bible School that was always popular was craft time. I'll admit, though, my God-given talents were rather limited in this area. There are only so many picture frames a kid can make out of Popsicle sticks before he cracks. Usually the Popsicle sticks cracked first, but I wasn't too far behind. Heaven only knows where all these Popsicle stick creations wind up after Vacation Bible School is over. I know I rarely had any desire to keep anything I attempted to make. I guess someone somewhere likes them. If you ever find yourself at a yard sale and see an intact Popsicle stick picture frame in a dusty box for sale for two cents, before you start trying to negotiate the owner down to one cent, if you want to ensure it was handmade in church, always make sure to look for the "Made in the VBS" label.

* * *

Whether at work, school, your place of worship, or around your community, there are many other wonderful ways to help others, and showing a little creativity along the way can produce some amazing results.

Perhaps you're into baking. If so, you could volunteer to prepare meals for those in need. You could even team up with other like-minded bakers and organize a food outreach and provide meals for the sick and shut-ins. Imagine how many lives could be touched!

Perhaps, like me, you're not into baking. If I tried preparing meals for others, we would have to organize a hospital outreach. I don't believe many people would like to taste my homemade Bubble Gum and Toast casserole. It's okay not to be good at something. I just learned along the way that you should learn what your strengths are and use your specific gifts and talents in such a way that the most people can be helped and the fewest amount of stomachs have to be pumped.

Perhaps you're an avid reader. If so, you could find someone in your community who is blind and offer to read to them. There are so many people in our world, especially people with disabilities, who are lonely and they need to know they are loved. Show them that love. I'll say it once more: "LET'S GET PEOPLE'S ATTENTION!!!"

To everyone reading this book, remember that you get one shot at life. Think outside the box and be creative! Don't be afraid to channel your inner "giant tooth" and make this world a better and brighter place to live, work, worship, and thrive.

To all the "giant teeth" out there, I salute you! Keep on keeping on, and no matter how much people laugh and point at you, keep your head held high and keep flashing those "pearly whites."

THE LIFE AND TIMES OF H 604

I'll start this next story with a little quiz. I'm going to give you a list of names and you tell me what they all have in common. Ready? Here goes: Mr. Nightmare, Blue Spooky, Darkness Prevails, Killer Orange Cat, and Hellfreezer.

If you guessed these are all nicknames for members of Congress, then you're wrong (maybe). These are actually the nicknames of popular narrators on YouTube who specialize in narrating horror stories. Some of the stories they narrate are true whereas others are works of fiction, but all these stories have the potential to be both scary and entertaining.

Often times when horror narrators post videos, there is a specific theme. For example, many narrators will do Scary Home Alone Stories or Scary Home Invasion Stories. As the titles suggest, these are stories about people who were home alone when someone tried breaking in and they were caught in potential life or death situations.

These are some of my favorite stories because not only are they scary, they can be very informative. If you listen to enough of these stories, you may even learn something that could someday save your life. The best stories in this genre are the ones where someone has broken into the house with the intent of either hurting or killing the homeowner. Near the end of the story just when it seems like all hope is lost for the homeowner, suddenly you hear the narrator utter those wonderful words: "Just then, I remembered where my father kept his gun collection upstairs." At this point, you know things will probably turn out okay.

I know gun ownership is a hot-button issue right now, but I believe any law-abiding citizen of sound mind has the right to own a gun to protect their life, their family, and their property. I'll admit I don't own a gun, though. Guns scares me. I'm a legally blind man with a liberal arts degree. The only gun that's safe for me to own would be plastic, pink, and shoots bubbles. Even then, I would still probably end up with a flesh wound.

So, for those of us who are gun shy, are there other alternatives? Sure. Another theme in many horror stories is Scary Encounters Where Dogs Saved the Day. If this scenario sounds better to you than owning a gun, you can always get yourself a good guard dog.

We had dogs in our family for years, but they were small lap dogs. Growing up, we had two dogs. The first dog we had was really smart. If someone had tried to break into our home, she probably could have scurried over to the phone and dialed 911. After this dog passed on, my parents bought another dog. This dog, however, was nowhere near as smart as our first one. As she grew older, she also developed cataracts in her eyes. If someone had broken into our home and I yelled "Attack!," this dog probably would have attacked me thinking it was the burglar.

As much as I love dogs, they have always made me nervous, especially large dogs. If my family ever decides to get another dog, though, I hope we end up with another smaller dog, like maybe a pug.

I love pugs. They are absolutely adorable. A pug can bring out the inner ninety-year-old grandmother in all of us. If you deliberately harm any dog, you should get jail time. If you harm a pug, however, you should immediately be sentenced to death.

Pugs are great, but let's get real. How well would a pug really do in protecting its owner if someone tried breaking into their home? Pugs aren't the best climbers, and those tiny little legs will only get them so far. If I'm upstairs in my house and I hear someone breaking in downstairs, I'm going to immediately lock myself in my bathroom and call 911. If I own a guard dog, I'm going to hope the dog will do what it's supposed to do and run down the stairs to attack the intruder. If I have a pug as my guard dog, however, I'm likely going to have to unlock the bathroom door and tell the 911 operator to hold on a second as I proceed to carry the pug downstairs and place it at the door to wait for the burglar to break into the house. If the burglar does break in, the best I know I could really hope for is the burglar gets frightened off because they mistook the pug for a tiny space alien or they heard the pug wheezing because of its sinus issues and thought it was rabid.

*   *   *

There are many other horror story themes out there as well. In no particular order, here are some of my personal favorites:

Scary Haunted House Stories: These are always a fan favorite. These are stories about frightening unexplained events that occur in people's homes. I won't go into the content of such stories, but I will say that if you want to avoid living in a haunted house, make sure there are NO Ouija boards anywhere in the home and NO Native American burial grounds anywhere under the home and you should be fine. If you still experience hauntings, please contact a Christian pastor for further assistance.

Scary Elevator Stories: Generally, these are stories where someone is trapped against their will in an elevator with either a psycho serial killer or someone who just ate a burrito from a vending machine moments before entering the elevator. Through these stories, you learn to survive either by using pepper spray or Lysol spray.

Scary Janitor Encounter Stories: Hey, somebody has to clean up that elevator.

Scary Airport Stories: These are stories about frightening encounters people have had on planes or in airports. The scariest stories in this category always seem to include the line, "And then we discovered our flight was being diverted to Atlanta."

Scary Hospital Stories: These are stories about hospital patients who claim to have seen the spirits of deceased patients roaming the halls of the hospital, were attacked by a fellow patient who was mentally unstable, or their doctor just informed them they are about to receive an injection and it's *not* going to be in their arm.

Scary Restaurant Stories: These are stories about frightening encounters people had while in restaurants. This includes stories of restaurant employees who had to fight off armed robbers or customers who turned out to be total psychopaths. Customers also have their own frightening restaurant stories as well, such as going out to breakfast, paying the bill, and realizing they actually just spent twelve bucks for a waffle.

Scary Beach Stories: These are frightening stories from beachgoers that include accounts of being attacked by mysterious sea creatures while swimming, finding severed body parts in the sand, or coming to the realization that none of the lifeguards on duty look anything like the ones on *Baywatch*.

Scary Jogging Stories: These are stories where people jogging had to fight off would-be attackers during their jog or after their jog they discovered the Krispy Kreme they usually go to was closed for renovations.

Scary Birthday Party Stories and Scary House Party Stories: I never worry too much about ever becoming the victim in these stories. Being unpopular has its advantages. If you don't get invited to the party, you can't get decapitated at the party.

Scary Paranormal Pet Stories: All I'll say about this category is that if your best friend's beloved pet dies, don't try to cheer them up by inviting them over to your house to watch *Pet Sematary*.

Scary Canadian Monster Stories: Yes, this is a thing, and there have been many encounters from our neighbors up north of unexplained creatures roaming around their country. The good news is we're talking about Canada, so even the monsters are pretty polite. If a monster shouts at someone to "Get out!," they make sure to say "please" and "thank you." Also, they're not really bloodthirsty. At worst, they're just maple syrup deprived.

Scary Australian Monster Stories: Okay, no jokes here. Australia is home to some MEAN creatures. If anyone from Australia claims they once saw a ten foot tall creature with twenty glowing red eyes walking on all fours with a tail that's actually a large venomous snake, I will believe them. What's even scarier is that even these creatures are afraid they could encounter a twenty foot tall creature with forty glowing red eyes walking on all eights with two venomous snake tails. If such a creature exists, it's going to be in Australia. I've heard in Australia when two creatures fight one another, it can get nasty. We're not talking King Kong versus Godzilla here, we're talking Walmart versus Amazon.

Scary Dogman Encounters & Scary Wolfman Encounters: I learned from these stories that the Dogman doesn't mind if he's mistaken for the Wolfman, but if you refer to the Wolfman as the Dogman, he *really* takes it personally. If you ever call him the Wiener Dogman, he'll show you how personally he takes it.

Scary Coyoteman Encounters: We know these are credible accounts because every time the Coyoteman was spotted, he was chasing after the Road Runnerman.

Scary Toy Stories: These are stories where people claimed to have supernatural encounters with old toys in their homes. I've yet to have any disturbing encounters with any toys we still have in our home. My sister has a Barbie collection, but I've never really feared they would come to life and kill us all in our sleep. We're talking

Barbie's here, and I think the dolls would be too afraid they would break a nail in the process.

Scary Musical Instrument Stories: These are stories about paranormal experiences people have had with musical instruments. Most of the time an old piano is the subject of these stories. In most cases, the piano starts playing music on its own. I'm sure that would creep some people out, but I'm sorry, I love creepy piano music. If the piano in my house starts playing on its own, I'm not fleeing in terror, I'm going to wait until it's done then ask it if it knows the opening theme to *Halloween*.

There's only one musical instrument that creeps me out, and it's the recorder. Those things are horrible! When Lucifer was kicked out of Heaven, I'm pretty sure he was playing the recorder at the time. When children play these things at school concerts, they're not just annoying their loved ones. For all practical purposes, they're putting their lips to a Ouija board and blowing.

Scary School Lockdown Stories: With so many acts of school violence, these types of stories really hit close to home for a lot of us. I was fortunate enough to attend a small fundamentalist Baptist high school and we never had any acts of violence. The closest we might have ever come to a lockdown was if a couple of Jehovah's Witnesses wandered onto the campus by accident.

First-Date Horror Stories: As a single guy, I usually listen to these to make sure none of the women who submitted these stories are talking about a date we went on. By the way, guys, here's a tip: When you're on a first date and she asks you what your hobbies are, don't include washing your hands or hiding on that list. If you do, you can rest assured, though, that there won't be any Second-Date Horror Stories.

Scary Witch Encounter Horror Stories: These are the guys' rebuttals to the women's First Date Horror Stories.

Scary Valentine's Day Stories: All you need to know is if you're in a relationship, don't forget Valentine's Day, and if you're single and not in a relationship, don't *remember* Valentine's Day, and you'll be fine.

Scary Bathroom Stories: These are stories about horrifying encounters people had while trapped in their bathroom. Popular stories include accounts of people barricading themselves in their bathroom during a home invasion or worse, coming to the conclusion that they never should have eaten a burrito out of that same vending machine when they finally escaped the elevator earlier that day.

Over the last couple of years I've really gotten interested in the horror genre, so I decided it might be fun to attempt to write my own horror story. I've been working on this story for a while now trying to perfect it so I can reach the maximum level of fright possible.

My story is entitled "My Trip to the DMV." As with any story about a trip to the Department of Motor Vehicles, this isn't for the faint of heart, so proceed with caution from here on out.

Here goes: Earlier this year, I had to renew my state ID card before my next birthday. My birthday was in a couple weeks, so I knew it was time to stop delaying the inevitable and make that dreaded trip to the DMV to get a new ID card.

Since I can't drive, my father drove me across town to the closest DMV office. We arrived at the DMV a couple hours after it opened because I thought by then it wouldn't be crowded. Once I arrived, I was quickly reminded there is really *never* a good time to go to the DMV. I was also quickly reminded that people as naive as me are generally the first ones to bite the dust in horror stories, so things weren't looking too good for me at the moment.

A few minutes after arriving, I stood at a desk just outside the main DMV office where I spoke to a woman who we will call "the Gatekeeper." I told "the Gatekeeper" why I was there, and she printed me out a ticket number and told me to have a seat in the waiting area until my number was called.

For this portion of the story, I now have a new identity. I am no longer Brandon. I am now "H 604." You can call me Mr. 604, or just H. I'm flexible. People say you're treated like a number at the DMV. Well, these days you're treated like a letter *and* a number. Uh, progress?

My first official act as H 604 was to walk back to the waiting area to sit down. I quickly realized my second official act was to stand indefinitely because there was nowhere to sit in the waiting area. As time went by, my fellow letter/numbers were called, and seats finally become available. Before I could sit down, however, I had to make sure it was just the right seat. The "right" seat is any seat where I don't have to sit next to any sneezers, wheezers, criers, coughers, itchers, scratchers, yellers, smellers, moaners, groaners, belchers, or barfers.

Finally, a couple seats became available in the back of the waiting area next to the wall. My father and I sat down. I took the seat closest to the wall which allowed my father to act as a barrier between me and the rest of humanity. He's not bothered by germs. He rarely gets sick and rarely worries about getting sick. He grew up in the country and to him, dirt was an afternoon snack. I envy him, really. He probably has much better immunity to germs than someone like me who avoids germs at all cost. He'll likely live to be a hundred and I'll probably get licked by a pug next week and die from the first reported case of Doggy Ebola in the U.S.

Like the naive person I was, I didn't think I would have to sit very long, so I didn't bring anything to read. I soon learned you should *always* bring something to read while waiting at the DMV. Popular suggestions include lifestyle magazines or a copy of *War and Peace.* You'll probably have time to read both.

So, there I was, sitting in the chair and just letting my mind wander. I started thinking about my upcoming birthday. I couldn't believe I would be turning thirty-eight. That's almost forty. That's a whole other horror story.

As I continued to sit, I began looking for *anything* around me that I could read. I even spent a large amount of time just staring at my ticket number. Sadly, it didn't take me long to read it. I read it again. Surprisingly, it didn't get any better the second time.

Time seemed to stand still, yet somehow, it still moved faster than me. Whenever someone was called, the letter and the number on the person's ticket were called over a loud speaker in the waiting room. I kept staring at my H 604 ticket and thought, *If they call A 604 before me, if I take the black pen I had in my pocket and put a little line over the top of the H, is there any possibility someone would actually fall for it?* Then, I realized that's not a very Christian thing to do. If Jesus had to wait at the DMV, He would never take a pen and change His ticket. Then, I realized Jesus wouldn't have to because He could just lay His hand on the His ticket and turn it into whatever number He wanted.

I began to wonder what else Jesus would do if He ever had to wait at the DMV. If I had to wait at the DMV while

Jesus was there, now *that* would be awesome! We know from the Bible that when Jesus was surrounded by crowds, He fed them. One time, He even fed five thousand people with just a few loaves of bread and a couple of fish. Since that's about how many people are waiting in the DMV at any given time, I think it's safe to assume lunch would be provided if Jesus showed up.

Jesus also healed the sick, so it wouldn't matter who you ended up sitting next to, because if they're not contagious, they're better off and now, so are you. If you were really fortunate, perhaps Jesus could even turn the nearby water fountain into a wine fountain, but I digress.

I was snapped back to reality when I heard over the loud speaker, "H 602, please report to Station 4." I think, *Yes, I'm almost there. It's almost over! Only a couple more numbers to go!* I figured, at most, only another forty-five minutes to an hour of waiting.

But then, tragedy struck. Instead of hearing, "H 603, please report to Station Whatever," I heard something along the lines of, "C 203, please report to Station Whatever."

NOOOOOOOOOOOOOOO!!!!!!!

I thought, *We've just gotten to the H's! We can't go back to the C's! The C's have had their moment in the sun, and now it's time for all the H's in the world to shine!* At this point I was getting pretty angry at the C's. How were they any better? Reluctantly, I calmed down and realized it doesn't do any good to compare myself to others. All

I could do was wait patiently and strive to be the best H possible.

Finally, after a minute shy of eternity, I heard those magic words, "H 604, please report to Station 4." Victory was finally mine! My time had finally arrived! As I stood up to walk out of the waiting room, there was a little spring in my step. Actually, upon further reflection, it may have been an uncontrollable muscle spasm brought on by sitting for so long. This didn't matter, however, because it was now MY turn!!

I quickly walked into the main DMV office, found my appointed station, presented the DMV worker with the needed documentation, and soon it was time to take my picture for my new ID card. They actually had me remove my glasses for the picture. Then, I was asked to face a little blue light in the direction of the tiny camera. Of course, being legally blind and not being able to wear my corrective eye wear, I had a hard time trying to find that pesky little blue light.

After an impromptu game of "Hot" and "Cold" with the DMV official, the little blue light was successfully located and my picture was taken. It turned out to be one of the best pictures I have ever had taken of me. The lady who took it might actually have a second career as a fashion photographer because on this day, H 604 was stylin'!

Finally, my trip to the DMV was about to come to a merciful end. I knew I would live to tell the tale. Of course, like with many other horror stories, there is always some plot twist at the end. As I was about to walk out, the question was raised about what was the best time to come to the DMV. Chills shot through me when I heard the DMV official's response: Call the office ahead of time and just set up an appointment.

It just goes to show that one person's horror story can be another person's comedy. In the end, though, I learned the DMV will always get the last laugh, and it doesn't get much scarier than that.

WHEREFORE ART THOU, JUDY WINSLOW?

Growing up, television was a big part of my life. At any given time, I would have at least thirty or so favorite TV shows and for good reason. Television was so much fun when I was a kid.

Do you remember when TV shows had catchy theme songs? I loved the theme songs. I could be in another room when the television was on, and just by hearing the first couple notes of the theme song, I knew exactly which show was about to start. Sometimes the theme song was the best part of the TV show. Even if I didn't watch the show, sometimes I just wanted to hear the theme song, and as soon as it was over I would change the channel. I'm ashamed to admit that I've probably memorized more TV theme songs than I have the hymns we sing in church on Sundays. If we ever had to start singing the hymns by memory, I'm certain I would start out singing *Just a Closer Walk With Thee* and end up singing the lyrics to

Three's Company. Personally, I'm waiting for the next Women's Sunday in the hopes we'll start the service off by singing the theme to *The Golden Girls.*

Even television commercials were fun when I was a kid, especially on Saturday mornings. Like most kids, I loved my Saturday morning cartoons. My favorites were *Garfield and Friends, Teenage Mutant Ninja Turtles,* and *The Real Ghostbusters.* Of course, I still preferred to watch my cartoons over the commercials, but if I was lucky, the commercials would be advertisements for new toys and action figures for the show I was currently watching, so I felt like I was still watching the show.

Commercials were very effective in getting kids hyped up about all the new "must have" merchandise related to their favorite cartoons. I think *The Real Ghostbusters* had the best commercials. I begged my parents to buy me the latest ghost-busting merchandise on many occasions. I had so many plastic ghosts of all shapes and sizes in my bedroom that it wasn't just messy, it was haunted. I'll never forget when I got the official *Ghostbusters* firehouse headquarters. I'm sure my father will never forget having to put that thing together, either. Halfway through that construction job, my father looked scarier than some of the ghosts on the show.

I remember one of the items that came with the firehouse was this can of slime-like substance. If I remember the commercial correctly, I think you poured the slime through a skylight in the roof of the firehouse to pretend like it was under attack by a ghost or something along those lines. For obvious reasons, my parents hated that can of slime and never wanted me to open it. For years, it just sat unopened on a shelf in an old pie safe in our kitchen. We had never even taken it out of the original plastic. Eventually, it got thrown out. I was okay with this until I looked online recently and discovered unopened cans of the slime were selling for around a hundred bucks!

For years, people have given me tips about making money. Some have said to enroll in a 401(k), whereas others have said invest in a Roth IRA. Here's my advice: DO NOT throw out the slime! You'll thank me later.

✳ ✳ ✳

There were so many great choices of television shows back in the Eighties and Nineties, and I was lucky enough to watch many of these shows when they first aired. If you were like me and loved scary TV shows, you had great shows like *Rescue 911* or *Unsolved Mysteries*. Robert Stack, the host of *Unsolved Mysteries*, had the scariest voice of any narrator I ever heard, then and now. Had Stack's voice been just one octave scarier, I truly believe he could have scared the Devil into salvation.

Another scary TV show, or I guess I should say semi-scary TV show, I loved to watch growing up was a show on Nickelodeon called *Are You Afraid of the Dark*? It was about this group of kids who called themselves "The Midnight Society." Each week, they would sit around a campfire and take turns telling a scary story that was played out over the course of the episode.

Because this show was targeted to kids, looking back, not all the stories were all that scary. Honestly, some were pretty corny in my opinion, but it was still a fun show that delivered just the right balance of age-appropriate fright. I always thought, though, that it would have been so awesome if Robert Stack would have made a guest appearance on *Are You Afraid of the Dark*? They could have had him play the father or grandfather of one of the kids in "The Midnight Society," and he could have narrated his own scary story for the group. By the time he finished speaking, those kids would have been scared spitless and would never spend another night in the woods again. They would have to change the name of the group to "The Mid-Morning Society."

Speaking of Nickelodeon, how many of us were lucky enough to watch Nickelodeon back in the Nineties when many felt the channel was in its Golden Age? Back in the day, Nickelodeon had some of the greatest original programs for kids that ever existed. I couldn't tell you what programs are on Nickelodeon today. I haven't watched the channel in years. Single men in their late thirties who regularly watch Nickelodeon tend to be questioned first by police during active criminal investigations. I will say, though, over the last few years I've seen a few clips of recent Nickelodeon shows as well as children's shows from other channels, and personally, my heart breaks a little for today's generation of younger television viewers.

Growing up, I watched fun shows like *Hey Dude*, *Salute Your Shorts*, *Welcome Freshmen* (my personal favorite), and who could ever forget *Clarissa Explains It All*? I loved the character of Clarissa Darling and her crazy family. Her father was an architect who designed weird-shaped buildings, and her mom always seemed to be torturing the rest of the family with her healthy cooking. I think this show was the first time I ever learning about the existence of tofu. It made me curious to want to try it and see how it tasted. Long story short, it did not become a fan favorite in my household. Looking back, I think the tofu they talked about on the show was part of the special "Just Say No" episode that was so popular back then.

As much as I loved Clarissa's family, my favorite character on *Clarissa Explains It All* was Clarissa's best friend, Sam. When he wanted to see Clarissa, he rarely knocked on her front door, but instead, climbed up to her second story bedroom window on a ladder and just came on in like it was the most natural thing in the world. As great as Sam was, though, I always hoped he would eventually get out of the habit of entering girls' bedrooms through an open window using a ladder. If he didn't, I feared that if Sam and Clarissa ended up attending the same college and living in the dorms, Sam would end up with a lot of explaining to do with the campus police.

Before I move on, I'll mention one more show from Nickelodeon's glory days that holds a special place in my heart: *The Adventures of Pete & Pete*. This was a show about two brothers, both named Pete, and the older

Pete's friend Ellen Hickle, who was a girl and a friend, but not a girlfriend. Ellen was a very relatable character. It seems like every girl I ever had a crush on growing up turned out to be my very own Ellen Hickle. (On a couple of occasions, they turned out to be my very own Ellen DeGeneres, but that's another story.)

There were other memorable characters on the show. There were Pete and Pete's parents. Their mother had a metal plate in her head which she used to pick up radio signals. Little Pete also had his own personal superhero, Artie: The Strongest Man ... In the World! If this were an audio book, that last sentence would be infinitely funnier, trust me.

The Adventures of Pete & Pete was a crazy fun show and really touched on what it was like to be a kid in the Nineties. The show was a perfect combination of realism and surrealism. In one episode, it's summer vacation and the family takes a trip to a nearby beach. The father is walking along the shore with his metal detector and it starts beeping. He gets excited and starts digging. Whatever it is, it's huge, and the rest of the family begins to help dig the object out. Long story short, the family ends up digging up a 1978 Oldsmobile in pristine condition. Apparently, the keys were still in the car because the family just drives away in their newly-found Oldsmobile.

As a kid, I remember thinking there is no way something like that would ever happen in real life. I later read somewhere that this show was filmed in New Jersey and possibly based on a town in New York, so perhaps finding a car buried in the sand is perfectly normal for the folks up there. So help me, though, if they opened the trunk and didn't find a skeleton wearing a three-piece suit, then I'm afraid this episode loses all credibility for me.

Another great episode was the one where Little Pete fakes being sick to stay home from school. He and Big Pete hatch a plan. Little Pete pays off a grocery store worker to give him a label off an expired can of tapioca pudding, and Big Pete puts the label on another can of tapioca pudding and throws it in the trash, making it look like Little Pete had unknowingly eaten some bad tapioca pudding the night before and now had mild food poisoning. The plan works, and Little Pete gets to stay home from school. It was a great episode, but I don't really know if pretending to be sick to get out of school is the best message to present to impressionable children. Little Pete should have taken it like a man, done a crossover episode with *Clarissa Explains It All*, and eaten some tofu at her house for dinner. There's a good chance that the next day, he would not have been faking it.

I loved comedy shows growing up, especially the sitcoms on the major networks. Back then, you made sure to be in front of the TV on Friday nights because that was TGIF night on ABC. These shows were so cool! You had great family shows like *Step by Step, Boy Meets World*,

Hangin' with Mr. Cooper, and one of my all-time favorites: *Perfect Strangers.* If you never saw *Perfect Strangers,* it was about these two guys named Larry and Balki. Balki was a shepherd from a fictional island in the Mediterranean called Mypos. One day, he shows up unannounced at the door of his "Cousin Larry" in Chicago. They had never met one another before, but Larry decides to let Balki live with him in his apartment. Balki knows virtually nothing about life in America, and Larry, a rather neurotic man, decides to take Balki under his wing. Do comedic hi-jinks ensue? Well, as Balki might say, "Of course they do. Don't be ridiculous!"

Perfect Strangers had some of the best physical comedy I ever saw on television. In one episode, Balki bakes a traditional Myposian dessert called Bibbi Babka. (To all the *Perfect Strangers* fans out there, please forgive any misspellings on my part.) So, Larry thinks the Bibbi Babkas are good enough to sell, and he gets a large order that has to be filled by a fast approaching deadline. Larry and Balki end up turning their apartment into a makeshift bakery. Balki knows there is a certain way to bake the dessert, but Larry insists on cutting corners so they can meet the deadline. They do meet the deadline, but just as Larry opens a box to inspect one of the the Bibbi Babkas, it explodes in his face. To their horror, soon the rest of the Bibbi Babkas explode. It is at this point that Balki tells Larry if the Bibbi Babkas are not baked in the traditional Myposian way, the Bibbi in the Babkas goes "boom." This remains one of the best moral lessons I have ever learned from any TV show from my childhood, and I carry it with me to this day.

As the series went on, Larry and Balki would eventually land great jobs, marry their beautiful blonde flight attendant girlfriends, move into a beautiful Victorian home, and became fathers. As Balki would say, "Now we're so happy. We do the Dance of Joy!"

Another show I loved on TGIF was *Family Matters*, which actually was a spin-off of *Perfect Strangers*. *Family Matters* was a comedy about an African-American family in Chicago named the Winslows who lived next door to this annoying but good-hearted teenager named Steve Urkel who seemed to leave a path of destruction anywhere he went, much to the annoyance of the poor Winslow Family. I watched *Family Matters* religiously for years and absolutely loved this show, but one thing about it has haunted me to this day.

The Winslow Family had three children. The oldest daughter was Laura, who for years, was the unwilling love interest of Steve Urkel. They also had a son named Eddie, who was usually equally annoyed by Urkel. There was also a third child, a younger daughter named Judy. Judy was never a huge part of the show and never got much screen-time, but she still was a presence.

Then, after a few seasons, Judy just suddenly disappeared from the show. You never saw her anymore and nobody spoke of her. I would watch an episode and think, *Well, maybe Judy will show up this week*. She never did, however. For whatever reason, she was literally written off the show like she didn't even exist. As a kid, I had a lot of questions about this. I was really worried about Judy. I thought this might be a good time to have a *Family Matters/Unsolved Mysteries* crossover episode where Judy got listed as a missing person or something.

For the remaining five seasons or so of *Family Matters*, life went on without Judy. Laura finally realized she loved Steve, and in the last season, they planned to be married. Then, the show got canceled. Fans like me were heartbroken. If the show had been renewed for one more year, there is no doubt in my mind there would have been a wedding episode. What's even more interesting is that I read somewhere that, had the show come back, there was talk they were going to bring back the character of Judy Winslow.

You know what? Forget Steve and Laura's wedding. If this rumor is true, I want to know how they would have brought back Judy. I guess that means she was still alive the whole time, so that was a blessing. We'll never know what happened for sure with Judy Winslow, but I had always hoped she just wanted to get away from Steve Urkel, ran away from home, and ended up living with a nice sitcom family over on CBS.

* * *

Another type of show I loved growing up were game shows. Game shows were especially fun to watch when you were sick and you got to stay home from school. My two favorite game show hosts were Bob Barker from *The Price Is Right* and Monty Hall from *Let's Make A Deal*. These two men helped more kids get back on the road to recovery than some pediatricians.

Bob Barker had this way of getting everyone in the audience so excited about the games. A contestant could be playing a game and make a guess on a prize that you could tell the audience wasn't too happy they made. This was when Bob Barker really shined. He would use this opportunity to get the audience hyped up. Bob would say to the audience, both at home and in the studio, something like, "Never before in the history of *The Price Is Right* has a contestant ever made a guess like this! Now, I know it looks like all hope is lost, but wouldn't it be *something* if this contestant is right?" The audience would get excited and start applauding. Bob wouldn't stop here, though. He was just getting warmed up. Then he would say something like, "Wouldn't it be *something* if this contestant defied all odds and won this game?" The audience would start shouting and applauding louder. Bob had everyone in the palm of his hand. Then he would say something like, "Never before in the history of *The Price Is Right* has this happened, and we may be about to witness something AMAZING!!"

By now, the audience could hardly contain themselves. Everyone watching would be on the edge of their seats. We were all in this together. Then Bob would say, "Show us the correct price!" If the price was wrong and the contestant lost, we all felt like we lost that day. If the contestant won, however, there was joy in the land! Only Bob Barker could make a contestant correctly guessing the price of chunky spaghetti sauce as amazing as Jesus walking on water.

Monty Hall had a slightly different approach on *Let's Make A Deal*, but still a good one. He made you feel like you had just walked into a carnival. He had this knack of making a contestant second guess every choice they made. They could choose Curtain # 1, but there might be an even better prize behind Curtain # 3. They could choose the large box on stage instead. If the contestant chose the box over the curtain, Monty might then offer the contestant five hundred dollars to NOT take the box. Then, he might offer them a thousand bucks NOT to take the box. Then maybe two thousand. If the contestant stayed with the box, they would then open it up and the prize could be anything from a new dinette set or a trip to Hawaii to an entire wardrobe made out of spaghetti noodles or a lawnmower made out of a goat. The latter prizes, were, of course, the "zonk" prizes. If you got "zonked," sadly, you lost.

No matter what game show I watched, it was always fun watching the contestants reactions when they won a prize, no matter how small it was. It was so great to see someone win a hundred bucks and a can opener and for a few precious minutes, they acted like all their problems were solved.

I still love game shows, but they just aren't as fun to watch now as they were back in the day. Back then, contestants would often go on game shows dressed in coats and ties and dresses as if they had just come from a job interview. Today, they often come dressed like they just left an all-night party at the beach. From the way they act, apparently there must have been a lot of heavy drinking at that party.

In addition to *The Price Is Right* and *Let's Make A Deal*, there were other game shows I loved watching. There was *$ale of the Century*. Anytime a game show used the dollar sign instead of the letter "S" in the title, you knew it was going to be epic.

In *$ale of the Century*, you had three contestants who were asked a series of questions by the show's host. For each question they answered correctly, they would get five bucks added to their "bank." Of course, the contestant with the most money in their bank at the end of the game would be the winner. What was cool about this show was periodically throughout the quiz round contestants were given the chance to buy prizes. They would show a prize, something nice like a new stereo system or a piece of jewelry or any number of other great prizes. Normally, such prizes would sell for hundreds or thousands of dollars. On *$ale of the Century*, however, the contestant might be offered the chance to buy that stereo system for ten bucks or that jewelry for five bucks.

Of course, if they bought the prize, that money was subtracted from their bank and this could mean they would end up losing the game if they didn't have the most money at the end. Some contestants jumped at the chance to buy prizes they were offered whereas others didn't give in to the temptation. Ironically, today many of the prizes that were bought for five or ten bucks that cost them the game years ago are now actually worth five or ten bucks. If watching *$ale of the Century* taught me anything, I learned about self-control, especially with money. For some contestants, their mindset was "Buy! Buy!". In the end, though, they had to say, "Bye, Bye," because they lost.

Another game show I loved was *Press Your Luck*. Like *$ale of the Century*, *Press Your Luck* was part quiz show where the contestants would answer questions and earn points. To me, this was the boring part of the show. The next round, however, was when they brought out the large game board with all sorts of cash and prizes … and the Whammies. Each contestant would take turns as screens would light up on the prize board. Whatever was lit up when they hit the buzzer was the prize they won. The mantra of many of the contestants during this round was "Big bucks! Big Bucks! NO Whammies!" If they landed on a Whammy, however, they weren't as fortunate.

Whammies were these little animated gremlin-like creatures that appeared on the TV screen and they had one purpose in mind: to steal all of the contestant's money. The Whammy would come on the screen by doing things like riding a shark or flying on a carpet or using roller skates. Sometimes the Whammies would play instruments, or dance, or even sing. I loved the singing Whammies as a kid. They actually had pretty great voices. I'll take a singing Whammy over Taylor Swift any day of the week.

Every time a contestant landed on a Whammy, they lost all the money or prizes they had earned. If they got four Whammies, they were disqualified from the game.

I'm not going to lie. As a kid, I LOVED the Whammies and I wanted the contestants to land on a Whammy so badly just to see what it would do. Sadly, *Press Your Luck* was canceled after only a few years on the air. I actually heard just recently that there may be plans on bringing a new version of *Press Your Luck* back to television, and I hope this is true. It's time a whole new generation got to see the Whammies in action.

I know it sounds bad, but I always felt sorry for the original Whammies. As a kid, I thought they would be sad their show was canceled. They always seemed so happy taking other people's money. I remember hoping they went on to find good jobs with the Internal Revenue Service.

* * *

As a kid, I watched contestants on game shows win a wide variety of prizes, but some prizes stand out. Does anyone recall that brief period in game show history where contestants had the chance to win ceramic dalmatians? I don't recall a lot about the Eighties, but were ceramic dalmatians part of a fad back then? Was this part of a weird period in American culture where the collective mindset in our nation was that a house is never truly a home without a ceramic dalmatian in it? How many of these ceramic dalmatians are still around today? I wonder if they found their "forever home" with the people who first won them or were eventually adopted by those guys from *American Pickers.*

Another prize I remember being popular on game shows was a food item called Rice-A-Roni, also known as "The San Francisco Treat." I know it's still around because in doing the research for this chapter, I went on the official Rice-A-Roni web page. I don't know if I have ever actually eaten Rice-A-Roni at any point in my life. I'm not even sure what the ingredients are. I think it's safe to assume there is at least rice and perhaps some other ingredient with "Roni" in it.

There was a time when if you won Rice-A-Roni on a game show, contestants seem genuinely happy, so it must be a quality product. I don't know if I would go as far as to refer to it as "The San Francisco Treat," though. I've been to San Francisco, and the best treat from that experience was making it out of there alive.

Of course, one of the best prizes you could ever win on a game show, past or present, is a brand new car. I will always love watching contestants win new cars. Ever since I was a little kid, I have always been a car nut. Cars fascinate me. Right now, my favorite TV commercial is that one for Carvana. You know the commercial, the one with the car vending machines? So help me, before I leave this Earth, I want to travel to wherever one of these car vending machines is located and try it out. I want to know if it's just like a regular vending machine. Honestly, what I really want to do is put the "coin" into the slot or whatever you do and hope I get to see a full-sized SUV get stuck halfway and just dangle there like a bag of potato chips just like in an ordinary vending machine.

As much I love cars, though, we all know now that some of the new cars they used to give away on game shows years ago really were not worth winning. Today, most cars are more reliable and much safer. They have airbags within airbags and come with "environmental protection" packages. When I was a kid, an "environmental protection" package meant it wasn't well-built and wouldn't start half the time you turned the key. If the car didn't run, it was less likely to pollute the environment.

Over the years, I've seen some not-so-nice new cars won on some game shows. On one game show I watched, I remember a contestant found out she was playing to win a brand new Chevy Chevette. I'm sorry, but Chevettes were not great cars, even when brand new. Why anyone would get so excited about winning one of these things is beyond me. I think between the bright lights from the studio and the audience cheering, I think she was temporarily blinded and had trouble hearing and thought the announcer said she was playing for a new Chevy **Cor**vette. That's the only thing that makes sense.

Love 'em or hate 'em, there was a time when you saw quite a few Chevettes traveling up and down the road. There were many high school parking lots filled with these cars. I remember in high school, I had a friend who drove a Chevette. One day, he was driving along and wound up hitting a deer. I'll never be able to prove this, but I think that deer knew his days on this Earth were numbered anyway, so when it saw my friend's Chevette coming down the road, the deer wanted to leave this world by doing at least one good deed and slamming headfirst into the car to put it out of its misery as well. The deer's efforts were in vain, however, because my friend had the Chevette repaired. The deer died, but the Chevette lived on.

Another car that was a popular prize on game shows back in the day was the Ford Pinto. What can you say about a Pinto that hasn't already been said in numerous court rooms by numerous lawyers?

Can you imagine being the grand prize winner on a game show back in the day? You've won the bonus round, and now you get to take home your very own ceramic dalmatian, a ten year supply of Rice-A-Roni, and you get to carry them home in your brand new Ford Pinto. So, afterwards you load up your Rice-A-Roni in the backseat, you buckle up your ceramic dalmatian in the passenger seat so you can use the carpool lane, and you start up your new Pinto for the very first time. Unfortunately, all of your Rice-A-Roni obstructs the view out of your back window, and as you're backing your Pinto out of the parking spot, you lightly bump into a telephone poll. Since this is a Pinto, we know what will likely come next:

KABOOM!!

So, now your new Pinto is engulfed in flames, and you have only a few precious seconds to unbuckle your seat belt and save yourself. You escape the car and run away, but you realize your ceramic dalmatian is still inside cooking with the Rice-A-Roni. You manage to pry open the passenger door and pull man's best ceramic friend to safety. The Rice-A-Roni can't be saved, though. Soon, the fire department shows up, but they have to wait to put out the fire. The Rice-A-Roni hasn't finished cooking yet.

There's one more car I want to mention, but I don't know if it actually applies to this list, and that's (drum roll, please) … the Yugo. I have tried to find videos online of game shows giving away Yugos as prizes, and honestly, I was unable to find a single video. It's like this car was so bad, TV game show producers knew if they tried giving Yugos away, their ratings would plummet. If, for example, a Yugo had ever been used as a prize on *Let's Make a Deal*, the minute the curtain opened and the contestant saw that Yugo, I feel quite certain they would have been silently praying, *Merciful God, please let that car be the zonk prize. I'd rather leave with nothing than leave with THAT!*

Nobody could make a Yugo look good. Even Bob Barker would have failed miserably. If they ever did try to give one away on *The Price is Right*, the minute the door opened and everyone saw the Yugo, all eyes would be on Bob Barker. I'm pretty sure the first words out of his mouth would have been, "Nah, I've got nothing. Let's call it a day."

Sadly, as the years rolled by, people like Bob Barker and Monty Hall finally decided to call it a day. *The Price*

Is Right and *Let's Make A Deal* continue on with new hosts, but for me, it's just not as much fun. To me, game shows were the most fun when you only got to watch them once in awhile. Today, because of my work schedule, I actually get to watch game shows most every weekday, and honestly, that bothers me. As a kid, I used to think it would be fun watching game shows every Monday thru Friday. As an adult who now has that option, I question the choices I've made in life.

* * *

For me, television has lost a lot of its charm. There are very few TV shows I enjoy watching these days. When I do watch TV, I often find myself trying to be the responsible adult and watching news programs because I feel like I need to know what's going on in the world. I'm quickly reminded that what does go on in this world is rarely ever good. If I turn on any cable news network, it seems like all I ever hear anymore are people from every side of the political aisle pointing fingers and yelling at each other that they're wrong. If I wanted to hear this, I could just watch an *All in the Family* marathon and at least then there would be a laugh track.

I miss the shows of my childhood. I miss family comedies where all the problems were resolved by the end of the episode. I miss the characters from these shows: the funny families who made us laugh, the wacky next door neighbors who made life more fun and, from time to time, imparted a little wisdom along the way. I miss the talking dinosaurs and the lovable space aliens. I miss the TV shows where despite all the fights and frustrations, people stuck by one another through thick and thin and loved one another no matter what. Even as a kid, I knew the characters on these shows weren't real, but I wish they had been. Today, with all the reality shows we've been forced to endure, I look at the "characters" on these shows and know that they are real, but I sure wish they weren't. We've gone from TV characters who we welcomed into our homes each week to ones who make us want to install alarm systems in our homes in the hopes of keeping people like them away from our families at any cost.

There's one image I've seen on more than a few TV shows for years, and it perfectly captures how I feel about the state of television and life in general. It's the image that appears on practically every TV show that is set in New York City. It's that always-magnificent image of the New York City skyline filled with the tallest buildings I've ever seen in my life. When I see this skyline in the shows from my childhood, I always seemed to see those two magnificent twin towers of what was once the World Trade Center before the terrorist attack on that solemn September day that claimed the lives of thousands of innocent people and shattered the innocence we once took for granted.

These older TV shows were a reflection of life in a pre-9/11 world. These shows made me happy. Life seemed better. People seemed nicer. Bad things still happened, but in many ways, the world did feel safer. Today, the newer shows set in New York City no longer have that same World Trade Center in its skyline. These shows seem darker and meaner. They depict a world that is increasingly dangerous and potentially deadly at every turn. Many TV shows now capture this mindset no matter what city the story line takes place. The settings change, but the fears remain the same, on screen for the characters and off screen for the rest of us who allow these images into our homes.

Despite the fears that TV brings into our homes, we continue to press forward. We get up in the morning and go off to work or school or our places of worship or go out to lunch with friends or run errands or volunteer in our communities. We ask God for His mercy and protection for us and the ones we love, and hopefully, we thank Him for every day we are given with our family and friends. We don't know what tomorrow holds, or if there will be a tomorrow, so hopefully, we do what we can to make today count. Then, after the day is done, we lock our doors, turn on our alarm systems, make sure our weapons are accessible, and settle down for a quiet evening in front of the TV.

DEAD LIFE

It had been a rough couple of weeks. Due to scheduling changes at work, my hours had been drastically cut. When I finally got two days in a row at the gas station, the first day consisted of heavy downpours and me without a rain coat. The next day consisted of the store doing a special one-day only sale and the feeling that everyone in town had decided to fill up their gas tanks before they left. This left me wishing my hours had been cut back just a little more.

The shift finally came to a merciful end and I returned home, exhausted and stressed. All I wanted was to sit down in front of the computer and relax for a few minutes. Of course, the first thing I saw when I went online was a story of a mass shooting from earlier that day at a retail store in Texas. Many dead. Many more injured. Not a lot of answers, but lots of disturbing images. I did what I always do in these circumstances: I prayed for the victims. Prayers like this have been a frightening part of my routine lately.

The next morning, I woke up, hoping this day would be better than the last. I turned the computer on, hoping to see something that would take my mind off yesterday's mass shooting. Well, what I saw did take my mind off it, because now I was seeing images of yet another mass shooting, this time at a mall in Ohio. Once again, many dead and many more injured. Still not a lot of answers, but no shortage of disturbing images of the victims. I prayed yet another prayer for the victims. The words of this prayer were virtually identical to the one I prayed yesterday, only the names of the locations had changed.

The day went by slowly. Outside, it was raining again and just all-around gloomy. Every news story online was depressing. I was determined to make the best use of my time because, yet again, I wasn't scheduled to work again for days, which meant I'd have too much time on my hands and not enough money in my wallet. I decided to take a break from all the misery and see how the stock market was doing. That proved to be a mistake. It had plunged seven hundred points over fears of a trade war with China. I knew my 401(k) was going to take a hit and feared my Roth IRA would now be a Roth DOA.

When I worry, I eat. My philosophy is "When life gives you lemons, sell the lemons and buy some doughnuts." I resisted the temptation, though, because days earlier, I weighed myself on the scale and discovered I needed to lose about fifteen pounds.

By now, I'm worried about the safety of my loved ones, the size of my bank account, and the size of my stomach. For years, I used to feel sorry for people who chose not to be informed about what goes on in the world. These days, I admire their blissful ignorance.

* * *

There are many ways I try to escape the problems of the world. I love solitude. The time I spend with my family and friends is special, but the time I spend with just myself is necessary. Sometimes when I'm walking through a store and see a snow globe on a shelf, I think how great it would be to live in a little snow globe all by myself where all the problems of the world seem to be on the other side. Then I realize, sooner or later, someone always comes along and shakes up a snow globe. I don't think I would want to live on an active fault line. The monthly insurance premiums would be a nightmare.

One way I like to temporarily escape is through YouTube. I love YouTube. I would like to think YouTube loves me too, because every time I'm on YouTube, it always seems to have just the right video recommendations I need to escape reality for as long as necessary.

There are so many great video choices on YouTube. For example, I love YouTube's seemingly endless selection of music videos. I have rediscovered more songs from my childhood and teenage years than I ever dreamed imaginable. Love it or hate it, Aqua, Ace of Base, and the Spice Girls will *never* die, at least not in my house.

If I want a little comedy, YouTube also offers me an abundance of choices as well. Some of my favorite videos are uploads of old TV sitcoms that people had saved on VHS cassette tapes. Despite many of these shows being hysterically funny, many weren't on the air long enough to warrant ever releasing them on DVD or Blu-Ray. And yet, we were stuck with twelve seasons of *Two and a Half Men*. Is there any limit to the cruelty this world has inflicted upon us?

Another type of YouTube video I love watching are old clips of Bob Ross, perhaps the greatest nature scene painter in my lifetime. To the person or persons responsible for posting all the great Bob Ross videos on YouTube, you have truly done the Lord's work. Bob Ross was an amazing painter and an all-around amazing human being. Whenever he painted, he would talk to the audience in perhaps the most calming voice I have ever heard on a television show. He was always encouraging his audience to paint along with him. Bob Ross wanted people not to be afraid to paint, because as he always said, we don't make mistakes, we have happy little accidents. I'm not sure, but I think "happy little accidents" only applies to painting, though. Twelve seasons of *Two and a Half Men* wasn't a happy little accident; in my opinion, that was clearly a mistake.

I also enjoy watching video clips of *Mister Rogers' Neighborhood*. *Mister Rogers' Neighborhood* was one of the greatest TV shows of my childhood. I watched *Sesame Street*, too, but I don't recall ever liking it as much as *Mister Rogers*. I watched *Sesame Street* more so because the "cool" kids were watching it, and I wanted to fit in with them. *Sesame Street* was like the *Beverly Hills, 90210* of the preschool set.

Mister Rogers was an amazing show for kids and really, adults, too. I realize now I get more from watching *Mister Rogers* at nearly the age of forty than when I was four.

As a kid, I would always get so excited whenever *Mister Rogers* was about to start. The opening piano music would start playing, and then you would see "the neighborhood." I used to love looking at the little model neighborhood that always appeared at the start of each episode. It started out with a close-up of some taller buildings, and then the camera would move and make you feel like you were walking down the street. My favorite part was seeing all the tiny toy cars that were spread out on the street. Seconds later, you "arrived" at Mister Roger's little yellow house. Soon, Mister Rogers would walk through the front door, singing "Won't You Be My Neighbor?" (Oh, how I wish I could have been Mister Roger's neighbor.)

Mister Rogers wasn't "in your face" like many kid shows. It was warm. It was gentle. In many ways, it was a quiet show. Mister Rogers showed kids it was okay just to enjoy the quiet and use your imagination.

Like most children, my absolute favorite part of *Mister Rogers* was whenever he brought out the little red trolley because we knew it was time for another trip to the "Neighborhood of Make-Believe." Those puppets and their human friends had some fun adventures in the "Neighborhood of Make-Believe," and we got to be a part of it, if just through our TVs.

As a kid, I never realized just how many of those puppets Mister Rogers provided the voices for, but now, it blows me away. A lot of us kids learned some pretty valuable lessons in the "Neighborhood of Make-Believe." We learned sometimes bad things happen and don't always get resolved quickly. We learned that sometimes they don't get resolved at all. Perhaps the greatest lesson we learned was that everyone needs good friends, and we should learn to be good friends ourselves. If only we could all live in such a neighborhood in this day and age.

Sadly, Mister Rogers left the neighborhood twenty years ago and left this Earth a couple years later. I hope when Mister Rogers passed away, the angels brought him up to Heaven in a red trolley. He is truly missed by those of us who loved him and what he stood for in his life.

When I get to Heaven, one of the first things I want to do is meet Mister Rogers. Then after I meet him, I want to sit down and draw pictures with him and watch him put on a puppet show. What a great start to eternity that would be!

* * *

Of course I can't write about YouTube without discussing all the original YouTube content. In recent years, many people who have their own channels on YouTube have become internet celebrities. Some have even made a good living from the revenue they have made from their YouTube content. Whatever you're into, you will probably find at least one YouTube channel that shares your interests.

I've already written about all the great horror story narration videos on YouTube, but I also love watching relaxation videos. One specific type of relaxation video I've discovered on YouTube is ASMR videos.

Don't know what ASMR is? Well, let's take a trip over to Mr. Wikipedia's Neighborhood and find out! So, ASMR, or Autonomous Sensory Meridian Response, is basically this really pleasant tingly sensation you can get starting on your scalp and moving down the back of your neck to your upper spine. ASMR videos are specifically designed to produce this tingly feeling on the viewer. Sadly, after watching a number of these videos over the last couple years, it appears I'm quite "tingle deficient," but I still turn to ASMR videos to help me relax. The creators of these videos, commonly known as "ASMRtists" have become very popular in recent years, and some of their channels have millions of subscribers and the numbers continue to rise.

There are lots of different ASMR videos on YouTube because there are multiple ASMR triggers. For some people, ASMR can be triggered through hearing someone softly speaking or whispering. In many ASMR videos, the ASMRtist will just be sitting there looking at the camera and they just quietly speak about how their day was or what is going on in their life or any other number of topics. Some ASMR videos are positive affirmation videos where the ASMRtist says kind things to the viewers watching. This could include saying such things as, "You are special," "You are loved," or "You are one in a million," and so on.

As odd as it may seem, ASMR videos have helped many people feel better about themselves and have even helped people deal with anxiety and other serious issues like PTSD. It should be noted, though, that many ASMRtists are not trained health care professionals so ASMR should not take the place of needed counseling or therapy.

I won't lie. At times I've wondered if I could ever cut it as an ASMRtist, but I don't think I could. I'm easily annoyed by people, and I could never successfully do a positive affirmation video. I would end up softly speaking into a camera and saying things like, "Just what the heck is wrong with you anyway? Why do you act the way you do? And just who in their right mind told you that you were one in a million? I know *I* sure didn't. If *you* are one a million and there are seven and a half billion people in this world, if my math is correct, you and about another seventy-five hundred people are in desperate need of a good kick in the butt!" As you can see, I don't think I could cut it as an ASMRtist. A good ASMRtist helps to relieve PTSD, he doesn't trigger it.

In addition to softly speaking and whispering, watching someone writing or drawing has also been known to trigger ASMR. In these videos, ASMRtists might draw or paint a picture, or simply take out a piece of paper and just write random numbers or words. Sometimes they might write a variety of sentences. Since I write and draw, these are some of my favorite ASMR videos, but not always.

For someone like myself who is obsessive-compulsive, if I watch an ASMR video of someone writing random words or sentences and they forget to use an apostrophe when it's so, so, SO clearly needed, relaxing isn't an option. If an ASMRtist is doing a drawing video, and they are coloring in a coloring book and they color outside of the lines, I can't stop staring at that little mark outside of the line. I know it doesn't belong there. I know God doesn't want it there. God gave us lines for a reason, and I truly believe the main reason is because He wants us to stay inside them! When you color outside of the line, you are doing more than frustrating me. You are disobeying God! You shouldn't be allowed to do ASMR art videos if you flunked out of ASMR art school.

There are many other ASMR trigger videos. Some videos are of people tapping and scratching various objects, though I personally find these annoying. Some videos are of face touching as a trigger. In these videos, the ASMRtist touches on or near the camera to make the viewer feel like they are touching their face. These videos always make me nervous, especially when the ASMRtist has long fingernails because I feel like I'm about to get my eyes clawed out. How is *that* relaxing?

Ear-to-ear whispering has been known to trigger ASMR in some people, so some videos are of people moving from one side of the screen to the other while they make random sounds. All these videos have ever triggered in me, however, is motion sickness. Other mouth sounds that can trigger ASMR are the sounds of people eating and chewing food. Yes, there are actually ASMR videos out there where viewers sit and watch other people eat for given lengths of time. My advice is don't watch these videos when you're dieting. Chewing sounds from other people's mouths always tend to lead to growling sounds in my stomach that are far too loud to ever be used in an ASMR video.

One very popular type of ASMR video is role-play videos. In these videos, the ASMRtist pretends to be doing some type of specific job while using various ASMR triggers throughout the video. I've watched ASMR videos where people pretended to be teachers, bank tellers, and interior designers, among others. Some popular ASMR videos are medical exam role plays where someone pretends to be a doctor or nurse. Some favorites in this genre include the ASMR eye exam or ASMR cranial nerve exam. The ASMR prostate exam videos, however, don't appear to have achieved the same level of widespread popularity.

Some ASMR role-plays are a little out there. In some videos, the ASMRtist will use animals to trigger ASMR, such as puppies, kittens, or rabbits. Now, you're probably saying, "Well, does the ASMRtist pretend to be a pet shop owner or a veterinarian and use the animals as props?" The answer is yes, but that's not the weird part.

Now, I'm not actively searching out these videos, but I know for a fact there are ASMR videos of people dressed up like animals who *act* like the animal in an attempt to trigger ASMR. This can include the person barking, meowing, scratching, or purring. I'm sorry, but I find this far more disturbing than I do relaxing. If I watch a video of someone acting like a dog, the only thing I'm going to think is, *Gee, I really hope that dude is housebroken.* I will say, though, if I ever do see a video of someone dressed like a cat and they cough up a hairball, I still might subscribe to their channel. Watching those types of ASMR videos might actually help me stay on my diet.

Some ASMR role plays *really* disturb me. By scrolling through ASMR playlists, I've learned there are more than a few videos of fortune teller role-plays or role-plays of tarot card readings or healing crystal sessions. I'm guessing there aren't many ASMRtists who ever attended seminary, either.

As a Christian, these types of videos disturb me and I avoid them. If I watch an ASMR video where someone starts off by saying something like, "Would you like me to read your palm?," my gut instinct is to shout, "No, but you can read my lips … You. Need. Jesus."

What are my final thoughts on ASMR? Well, I think some of it's very good, some of it's very weird, and some of it, in my opinion, is very dangerous, especially to people who are looking for peace in places where there is no peace, only destruction.

When it comes to ASMR role-plays, I would suggest watching some of the ASMR Bible study role-plays. I've watched some good ones. Ultimately, though, no amount of relaxation videos will ever top the peace you get from having a relationship with God in your life. For true peace, the world needs God's ASMR: **A**ll **S**inners **M**ust **R**epent.

*   *   *

Now that I've discussed YouTube videos that can give you tingles, let's talk about another type of video that can give you chills. I'm talking about urban exploration videos. Just like ASMRtists, urban explorers have become a lot more mainstream in recent years. Who are urban explorers, you might ask? Well, you know how in every town or city there is that one abandoned building you drive by and always think, *Gee, I wonder what's in there?* Well, urban explorers are the people who have the guts to enter those buildings and find out. Now, thanks to YouTube, we can watch them explore from the comfort and safety of our homes. It might not be as much fun as being there with them, but at least you won't have to worry about getting a tetanus shot … or a gun shot.

I have never done any urban exploration myself, but by now, I've probably watched at least a couple hundred or so YouTube videos of urban explorers doing their thing.

I don't like to brag, but I've become quite "the armchair expert" of urban exploration. Here now are some of the most important lessons YouTube has taught me about urban exploration:

Be Prepared: There are risks to urban exploration. When you walk into an abandoned building, you don't know what you will encounter. Abandoned structures can be very unsafe. You could be walking into a building filled with broken glass and other kinds of debris. You never know when that ceiling above you could become a floor. If you're not careful, you might end up dying as a rug. Also, a lot of abandoned buildings are filled with mold and mildew and you could easily get sick if you breathe in enough of it. A good urban explorer knows these risks, and will make sure he or she has the right supplies. It reminds me of those verses in the Bible about putting on the armor of God. You know, the ones about having such things as the "belt of truth," the "sword of the Spirit," and the "helmet of salvation." It's sort of similar for urban explorers, except in this case, you should be using the "flashlight of illumination," the "boots of stability," and the "respirator of purification." Oh, you also may run into people who are living in those abandoned buildings who will not take too kindly to your being there, so you may also want to bring along the "mace of intimidation." Also, if possible, it's probably a good idea to have permission from the person who owns the building before you go exploring, because if you don't have permission and the police catch you, you could be the recipient of the "citation of trespassing," or worse, be led out of the building wearing the "handcuffs of restraint."

The Buddy System: While you can go urban exploring by yourself, it really is better to take along at least one other person. It can be a whole lot safer. Many of the urban explorers on YouTube know this. I think watching videos of at least two people exploring are actually more fun because it makes for some good conversations. You can listen to the two explorers bounce things off one another like, "How long has this place been empty?" or "What do you think this room here was used for?" or "Did you just hear someone upstairs shouting, "Get out or I'll kill you!!"? At this point our intrepid explorers know that they don't want to be the recipients of a "certificate of death," so they know it's time to hit the road.

Curb Appeal: Not all urban explorers go into abandoned buildings. Some choose to stay outside and film what they see on the outside. Some videos I've seen are from people who mounted cameras on the dashes of their cars and filmed what they saw as they drove around areas with numerous abandoned structures. Some of the areas they drive through are industrial or commercial areas filled with everything from countless abandoned warehouses and factories to residential areas filled with block after block of abandoned houses.

The residential areas are always some of the most depressing areas to see featured in such videos. It's always sad to see someone driving through what was once a beautiful neighborhood with once-beautiful homes that at one time were occupied by loving families. Today, many of those families are long gone. The homes they lived in are now abandoned and left to rot. Windows are broken or boarded up. The grass hasn't been mowed in ages. Some homes are covered in graffiti or burned out. Sometimes the entire street looks like this. At times, the person filming the video will provide their own commentary of what they are seeing as they drive along and how they feel about it. Other times, they remain silent and let the camera quietly capture all the depressing images as they allow the person viewing the video to make their own judgment call as to how things got this bad for such a once-thriving neighborhood.

It's easy to make judgment calls, especially when you don't know the facts. When I watch videos like this, I see all the abandoned homes and shake my head. Then I see the homes in the neighborhood that aren't abandoned and people still reside there. Many times these homes aren't in much better shape than the abandoned ones on either side of them. I get frustrated. I wonder if the people who live there are doing anything to try to get their neighborhoods and community back on track. Did they ever try? Did they ask for help and not get the help they needed? Did they just stop caring? It makes me wonder what needs to be done to get people to start caring again before it's too late.

Just as my frustration over the contents of the video is about to boil over into anger, that's when I see it: that one house. It's the one house where it's not only evident someone lives there, they take pride in living there. The lawn surrounding the house is neatly mowed, despite all the unkempt lawns that surround it. It's the one house where you know the cars in the driveway have been recently washed and are clean as they sparkle in the light of the sun. It's the one house where the trash is in the trash cans and not on the front lawn.

The house is beautiful. It may not be big or expensive, but it's clearly a home that has been well-cared for by its owner. The house has a fresh coat of paint. Sometimes there may be a little garden on the side of the house filled with colorful flowers. There might even be an American flag waving proudly from the front porch.

It's the house of the person or people who still care about where they live. Perhaps they can't afford to move out of the neighborhood. Perhaps they can, but choose not to because it's where they grew up and this is where they choose to make their home. Whatever the reason, it's obvious they are making the most of what they have. They may not always have the money, but they sure have the pride.

Sometimes when I see these homes in the videos, I say a prayer for the people who live in the house. I don't know them and know I'll never meet them. Yet, they inspire me. They inspire me not to give up, even when everyone around me is giving up. They inspire me to make the most of what I have been given and take pride in not only where I live, but also, pride in who I am and how I live.

May we pray these men and women continue to lead by example and give their neighborhoods the much needed care and attention they desperately need. May we pray that the day comes when these good people will once again become the norm in their communities and are no longer just the exception.

Dead Malls: The first time I ever heard the term "dead mall" was on a YouTube video from a talented filmmaker named Dan Bell, though I couldn't tell you if Bell coined the term. Dan Bell created a series of videos about dead malls, which refer to shopping malls that have already closed or have so few stores still in business that it's likely they will soon close. The retail industry has changed over the years, and shopping malls have lost much of their popularity. As Bell has alluded to in his videos, and others have commented on after watching them, there once was a time when the local shopping mall was the happening place to be: to shop, to work, to date, and perhaps even to fall in love. This was especially true for the younger generations who made their local mall a huge part of their lives.

Sadly, thanks to such things as the rise of online shopping and the fact many shopping malls are dealing with rising crime rates, many of these once-popular destinations have long since fallen out of fashion. Dan Bell knew this, so he created what he calls the Dead Mall Series on his popular YouTube channel, *This is Dan Bell.*, where he has traveled to shopping malls around the country over the last several years and filmed what he saw. What he has seen, and from what we can see from his videos, are often times large malls filled with only a small amount of shoppers and many, many closed stores. From the first time I saw a Dan Bell "Dead Mall" video, I was fascinated by dead malls.

It turns out other YouTubers share Bell's fascination, because since first viewing his work, I've discovered other talented filmmakers with channels on YouTube who have devoted much time and effort to filming dead malls all over the country. These videos have helped create many dead mall enthusiasts. Many people are so inspired by these malls that they make pilgrimages to see them in their final days before they close or perhaps are even demolished.

When you have watched as many dead mall videos as I have, sometimes facts tend to blend together, but through my three favorite YouTube channels, *This is Dan Bell.*, *Ace's Adventures*, and *Retail Archaeology*, here are just a few of the things I've learned about dead malls:

Massage chairs: In many videos of dead malls, you often find a number of empty massage chairs throughout the mall. There are massage chairs in busy malls, too, but in dead malls they tend to be more noticeable. I guess the good news for shoppers in dead malls is if you get tired from walking around trying to find a store that is still open, you can rest for awhile in pretty much any massage chair you want. Take your pick.

Charter Schools and Churches: As many businesses have moved out of dead malls, others have moved into these locations. Two popular types that have found room in many dead malls are small charter schools and storefront churches.

I imagine going to school in a dead shopping mall would be pretty depressing, but it would be awesome to attend a school in a busy mall with tons of stores around you. Instead of having lunch in a boring cafeteria, you could just mosey on over to the food court and take your pick of the junk food genre of your choosing. On top of it, if that food court has a Chick-fil-A in it, well, I don't think I have to tell you what I would be eating Monday thru Friday.

Of course, you would need to burn off all those extra calories, but that's okay, because a P.E. Class in a crowded mall would be great, too. You could run laps around the mall while annoying shoppers at the same time. In a dead mall, there wouldn't be many shoppers to annoy as you ran, but perhaps you could find a mall walker or two and challenge them to a foot race. If they accept, though, be careful. They may look harmless, but they can be deadly. You would need to constantly make sure they weren't trying to trip you with their canes. The average age of many mall walkers is about ninety, and you know they didn't make it this far in life by playing fair.

Attending a church in a mall could be cool, too, but again, I would want to be in a busy mall with lots of people and stores. I wonder what it would be like to attend church in a mall? The first question I have is do these churches use traditional wooden pews or would they take advantage of all those massage chairs?

Can you imagine the outreach opportunities available to mall churches? If there is a mall church out there centered between a Spencer's and a Hot Topic, that congregation will have more opportunities to witness to lost sinners than they'll know what to do with. Of course, most churches like to take mission trips to far away locations, like Haiti or the Dominican Republic. Sadly, many mall churches may not have the financial resources larger churches have, so they might only make it as far as Banana Republic.

Let's not forget one of the best features about attending church in a busy mall. Yep, I'm talking about the food court again. Imagine it. The Sunday service is about to come to an end, the preacher says "Amen," and now it's just a one-minute walk over to the food court. Of course, on Sunday you wouldn't have Chick-fil-A available for an option, though. So close, yet so, so far.

Anchor's Away: From watching dead mall videos, I've learned just how important anchor stores are to the life of a mall. In many malls, anchor stores, which you usually access from the exterior of the mall, are usually large and well-known stores known for carrying popular brands of merchandise. Some of the most popular anchor stores that have found homes in American malls are stores like Sears, JCPenney, Macy's, and Toys R' Us. Many of these anchor stores have been in business for decades and often provide much of the foot traffic to the smaller businesses that you can only access from the interior of the mall. Many times these include smaller national chains of businesses or local mom and pop stores such as antique shops, music stores, shoe repair stores, and so on.

Unfortunately, in recent years many of the companies that have brought anchor stores to malls haven't always made the wisest business decisions. Many of these companies have now closed their locations at many shopping malls. As they close and fewer customers have reason to come to the malls, the smaller businesses within the malls now often struggle to stay afloat. As Dan Bell and others have shown, this is the perfect formula for creating a dead mall.

I remember when I was a kid when my parents would drag me into these types of anchor stores for some horrible task like back to school clothes shopping. They pretty much had to bribe me with the promise that before we left, if the store had a toy aisle and I was good, there might be a new Hot Wheels or Matchbox car in my future. This made shopping with my parents so much more bearable. If someone had told me years ago that many of these stores would now be closed, I would have laughed. Today, nobody is laughing. Just like my childhood, I know many of these stores are never to return. All that's left are the memories.

* * *

As we continue to witness the demise of these once-popular anchor stores and the malls they once helped fill with shoppers, we are left with a surprising moral lesson. We are reminded how everyone needs strong anchors in their lives. Just as malls need strong anchor stores to survive, families also need strong anchors. They need caring and loving parents and grandparents and aunts and uncles who will stand firm and do what's right so the children in their care grow up to become responsible adults who will someday become strong anchors of their own families.

Churches also need strong anchors. They need pastors, deacons, and Sunday School teachers who lead by example and help equip others with the skills they need to lead Godly, moral lives. A church without strong leaders will never survive in this dark world. There are plenty of people out there to fill the pews, but they must first come through the doors. They can't come in if the doors are locked and there's no longer a church there to meet their needs.

Finally, communities need strong anchors. The cities and towns of our nation need men and women who care about where they live. They need servant leaders who put the needs of others ahead of their own. Contrary to popular belief, humility isn't a sign of weakness, but in fact, a sign of true strength. May we seek to elect leaders who look to God for this strength.

As this chapter comes to an end, may we take a few moments to reflect on the past. May we not only reflect on the past of our stores and shopping malls, but also on the past of our nation. America is a nation that was founded on strong Judeo-Christian values. For many years, these values served as the anchors in the lives of many. Today, these same Judeo-Christian values feel less like anchors and more like the stores inside a dead mall. The foot traffic just isn't there anymore and many fear the mall is about to close for good. Perhaps the concept of a "dead mall" doesn't scare you, and that's fine. But does the concept of a "Dead America" scare you? It should. If we're not careful, the day may very well come in our lifetime when this once great nation ceases to exist, and what has moved in to occupy the space will certainly make us all wish we had done a little more shopping while we still had the chance.

THE MOST MEMORABLE "FS" FROM MY SCHOOL DAYS

At the time I'm writing this, it's been over twenty years since I graduated from high school. It just seems like last week when I, along with the rest of the graduating class of 1999, turned our tassels from one side to the other and were turned out into the real world. I never thought I would be writing about it twenty years later. For one thing, I graduated just a few months before Y2K was supposed to erase all the computers and send us back to the Stone Age. I'm sure more than a few people thought we'd be living in caves by now and the Internet would have been replaced by the use of carrier pigeons. At this point, the closest thing we would have had to a computer virus would be an outbreak of bird flu.

Growing up, I had a love/hate relationship with school. Learning was fun when I was learning something that I wanted to learn. I remember in the first grade when my class started to learn how to write in cursive. I felt so grown up. Do they even still teach cursive writing in schools anymore? Now that kids are glued to their handheld computer tablets, I think cursive has gone the way of ancient hieroglyphics.

I was a pretty good student. I always attended smaller, Christian schools growing up, and I received a good education and the personal attention I needed because of my vision issues. I graduated high school at the top of my class, which is pretty easy to do when there are only four people in the senior class. I went to college and earned a business degree. I went to graduate school and earned a Master's in Liberal Studies. I've now been working as a gas station attendant at a member's only warehouse club for nine years. Do you know what they call someone who earns a Master's in Liberal Studies and ends up working at a gas station?

Lucky.

Seriously though, as I was preparing to write this chapter, I tried to recall what my fondest memories from my school days were. I decided to compile a list of the things I liked the most about school, and interestingly, they all begin with the letter "F," as in "For anything not schoolwork related." (Thankfully, none of these "F"s ever found their way onto any of my report cards.) Now, for your reading pleasure, here are the most memorable "F"s from my schooldays:

Fire Drills: I LOVED fire drills when I was in school. Whenever I would be sitting in class and, all of a sudden, we would hear the sound of a whistle or the fire alarm, we knew we had just mere seconds to spring into action and evacuate the building. It was exciting. No matter which school I was attending at the time, fire drills were always taken very seriously. Remember, I'm talking Christian schools here. For us, fire drills were more than just learning how to escape from a building on fire. They were metaphors for escaping the eternal flames of Hell. After we made it safely outside, our teachers would then make us all line up in neat rows on the playground so they could do a headcount to make sure we were all out of the building.

My favorite fire drill memory was back in the sixth grade. At some point during our morning classes, we heard the fire alarm go off. Soon, we were quickly exiting the classroom and we made our way outside to our designated location. After we were all outside, a headcount was taken, all were present and accounted for, and soon, we were all headed back inside. No problem.

Later that day, though, it got interesting. Several hours later, we were back in class when, much to our surprise, the fire alarm went off yet again. Keep in mind we had just had a fire drill earlier that day, and we all knew it would be awhile until our next one. So, this left many of us with the "burning" question: Was there really a fire this time? Isn't it funny how when you're in panic mode, you can always smell smoke whether or not there's any smoke to smell?

Maybe I shouldn't admit this, but there was this little part of me that really wanted it to be a real fire. I'm sorry, but I don't know of a kid alive who hasn't fantasized at least once about their school burning to the ground. Of course, I didn't want to be in the school if it did burn to the ground, so I hauled my butt out of that classroom as fast as I could. Once again, we made it to our designated spots on the playground and another headcount was taken. Thankfully, there had been no fire, but it was soon discovered a student had pulled down the fire alarm. After all the headcounts that day, we all knew at least one head was going to roll.

Now, I never found out exactly why this kid decided to pull down the fire alarm. The story I later heard, and let me stress this is purely a rumor, was that he was standing in the hallway, minding his own business, when suddenly, he was overcome by the power of the Holy Spirit. He lost control of his body and began dancing wildly in the hallway. As he was dancing, he was waving his hands in the air, and in the process, accidentally pulled down the fire alarm. (I suppose in a Christian school it's possible a scenario like this could unfold from time to time.) I couldn't tell you if there was any truth to this story, but I can safely say that our teachers and the principal were certainly overcome by the power of the Holy Spirit that day when they didn't succumb to the temptation to strangle this kid.

Field Trips: Part One: I remember I went on some awesome field trips back in elementary and middle school. As a self-proclaimed freak of all things automobile related, I was just as excited about how we were going to get to our appointed destination as I was about being there.

For most schools, there were generally two options. Your class either went by bus, or some of the parents took a day off from work and drove you and your classmates in their own cars. The school I attended at the time had no buses, so we went with the second option.

When you're a kid of a certain age, it was vital to ensure you and your friends rode together in the same car, and just as important, you had to make sure it was the "cool" car. When I was a kid, though, the choices for the "cool" car were usually a first-generation Ford Taurus, a first-generation minivan, or a ten-year-old American made station wagon large enough to fit your entire class, your teacher, and the full-size aquarium in your classroom with room to spare. So, of these choices, which one was the "cool" car? The answer, of course, was the station wagon. I'll explain why momentarily.

First, let's talk about station wagons. Back in the day, these cars were tanks that could have been used for military service. They were often covered in acres of fake wood paneling and at times, had more bumper stickers on them than they had bumpers. Plus, they were long, and I mean L-O-N-G.

So, why would such a vehicle be considered cool? Simple. If you and your friends got to ride in one, you might get assigned to ride in the back seat. I don't mean the back seat right behind the front seats. I mean the "back" seat, also known as the third row seat. What made the third row seat in an old station wagon so cool to ride in on a field trip? Easy. You got to ride BACKWARDS!

Riding backwards in a station wagon was awesome! This was because it was a simpler time where children were under the misguided assumption that the adult driving the station wagon would be unable to see them or any immoral or illegal activity they were currently engaged in while sitting backwards in the third row. On many field trips from my era, countless children, specifically elementary and middle school boys, proudly sat backwards as they made rude faces and hand gestures to passing cops, truckers, or motorcycle gangs alike. How any of us ever made it to wherever we were going without getting run off the road or shot at by all the motorists we annoyed is nothing short of a miracle.

Field Trips: Part Two: Looking back, I remember that most of the field trips I went on were pretty awesome. Over the years, my class and I took tours of a local television station, a plantation home, and even a nuclear power plant.

My favorite field trip was in the fifth grade. It was an overnight trip. At the age of eleven, an overnight trip is a big deal. I remember we left school very early in the morning and traveled across the state to a large zoo and spent the day there. Then after leaving the zoo, we traveled to another part of the state and went to a planetarium. We spent the night in a motel, and early the next morning, we traveled to the state capital to take a tour of the capital building and a museum before returning home. As any kid from that era will tell you, it didn't get much better than that.

Since our school was so close to the coast, we also toured a historic battleship in a nearby city and even took a couple trips to the beach. Of course, no beach trip would be complete without taking your shoes off and getting your feet wet in the surf. The first time my class went to the beach we were able to do just this. Just a few minutes of splashing around in the water was as much fun to us as the whole overnight trip had been. The second time we went to the beach was for a science project of some kind, I can't recall any specifics. I do remember, though, that our teacher made it very clear that this beach trip was strictly business, and we were <u>not</u> to remove our shoes and walk in the surf.

Of course, like the wonderfully resourceful kids we were, we still found ways to get out feet wet. We were just smart enough not to take off our socks and shoes. If I recall correctly, our collective excuse was that we were standing on the beach, eagerly obeying our teacher's command not to walk in the water when suddenly, a giant wave snuck up from behind and attacked us without warning. Our teacher, not being an idiot, didn't believe a word that came out of our wet, sandy mouths. Thankfully, we were so close to the end of the school year she didn't have the energy to punish us.

As much as I loved field trips, not every field trip I went on was always fun. I recall the time in elementary school when my class took a trip to the woods.

I don't like the woods. Woods scare me. In some parts of the country, the woods can be spooky. Here in the South, our woods can be pure evil. We are home to some of the most deadly creatures known to man. Even the dirt is venomous.

Do you know who I blame for all the dangerous creatures that lurk in Southern woods? I blame Noah. In the Bible, it was written that Noah was instructed to bring a male and female of each animal into the ark so they could be saved from the upcoming flood and later repopulate the Earth after the flood.

God forgive me, but I really wish Noah had "forgotten" to put a few certain animals on the ark. These include all snakes, fire ants, ticks, and cockroaches. If these animals had never made it into the ark, Southern woods would be so much safer. I will say, though, I have never actually seen a cockroach in the woods. I believe their native habitats are garages, kitchens, and my bathtub.

God forgive me yet again, but when I get to Heaven, I want to find out where Noah is hanging out, sneak up on him from behind, and just slap him upside his head. I know that sounds harsh, but they say in Heaven you feel no pain, so Noah wouldn't be hurt, and I know I would feel a lot better, so why not?

Let's get back to my adventure in the woods. I honestly can't remember why my class took a trip to the woods that day, but I do remember we had lunch there. I was on guard the entire time for ticks, snakes, and also, tick snakes, a frightening animal rumored to be half tick/half snake. (This is the South, and I know the tick snakes live among us.)

I'll never forget lunch that day. We chose a little clearing within the woods to eat, and I spent most of the lunch on guard for tick snakes. Every few seconds, I would check in all directions to ensure I wasn't going to be the victim of a tick snake sneak attack. What was worse, I had a loose tooth that was about to come out at anytime. I think we all know what happened next. As I was chewing on the fruit snack dessert my mom had packed in my lunch, that pesky tooth decided that now would be the perfect time to leave my mouth and make its presence known for all to see.

So, not only did I have to contend with the tick snakes, but now I had a tooth in my hand I had to contend with as well. That's a whole lot of contending for a young person. I was now even more worried because I had always heard tick snakes like to feed on human teeth. To them, it's like a vitamin supplement. I knew I had no choice but to protect not only myself, but now my tooth as well, because it was vital that both the tooth and I made it out of the woods safe and sound so I could return home and place it under my pillow for the tooth fairy. For all this hard work, I was hoping the tooth fairy would generously compensate me for my effort. A lousy quarter under my pillow wasn't going to cut it this time. I wouldn't settle for anything less than a timeshare in Myrtle Beach. The tooth fairy had other ideas, however, and I think I ended up settling for fifty cents. Someday that tooth fairy is going to stick her hand under a pillow and get chomped by a tick snake, and when it happens, she better not come crying to me about it.

As bad as the field trip to the woods was, I actually went on one much worse. Once, in the fourth grade, my class took a guided tour of the medical lab at a local hospital.

Let me preface this story by telling you how much I hate germs. I hate being around sick people or any item that may have come into contact with sick people. Hospitals are not popular hangouts for us germ freaks.

I can't remember too many details from the trip to the medical lab. Repressing memories for thirty years tends to do that to you. What I do remember was arriving at the hospital and being escorted by our guide to the medical lab. Once we walked inside, I remember seeing a bunch of people at different tables wearing "medical clothes" doing what I can only describe as "medical stuff." The class stayed together when we walked around the lab, and from the start, our guide gave us the following warning: DO NOT touch any of the medical waste bags that were stationed around the lab.

Let me set the scene up for you. I'm a legally blind, germaphobic fourth grader who has been known to bump into things in places I've been a million times before, and now I'm being asked to walk around a crowded medical lab where I don't know where anything is and at the same time, avoid coming into contact with any of the numerous medical waste bags that I may or may not see until I get a fraction of an inch away from it. At this point, I'm praying for a miracle and hoping the next field trip we go on will be to a therapist's office.

As the tour continued, we also had to watch a demonstration of someone giving blood. Now, if germs are my number one fear, needles and the sight of blood are coming in for a tie for second place. I remember one poor girl in our class was about to pass out from watching and she was escorted outside. Oh, how I envied her!

I remember thinking that if I had known she was about to pass out, I could have been the hero and run to her aide to catch her in time. Then I remembered with my luck on the way over to help her, I would likely have tripped over my shoes and fallen face first into the nearest medical waste bag. I probably would have ended up walking out of there with a tail or an extra leg, which might have been okay if that extra leg helped me walk out of there a little bit faster.

When we finally left the medical lab later that day, I hoped on the way back to school we could stop and do something a little less stressful to take our minds off our trip, such as an impromptu visit to a roadside tick snake petting zoo.

Films: Does anyone remember being back in school, sitting in class bored out of your mind, when suddenly your teacher announced, "Tomorrow instead of our usual lesson, we're going to watch a film." Suddenly, the storm clouds began to roll away and you could see the faint glow of a rainbow on the horizon.

A film! You were going to watch a film! You were so excited that you just learned you were going to watch a film that you didn't even hear what the film would be. For all you knew, it was going to be an hour-long instructional film on how to effectively watch grass grow and paint dry simultaneously, but that was okay because it was still a film. As kids all knew, once the film started, all learning ceased to exist.

Fast forward to the next day. You were back in class, filled with excitement and anticipation. You and your classmates knew that in just a matter of seconds, there would be a knock on the classroom door. The teacher would open it, and then, you would all see one of the most beautiful sights imaginable to a kid: the sight of someone wheeling in the largest television cart you ever saw in your life with a TV on top, and just below that, a VCR.

For all the younger readers, a VCR (or video cassette recorder) was this amazing device where you could watch various films and TV shows on these things called video cassettes. Some of the earliest VCR models were as large as encyclopedias (that ancient book used to look up information that reigned supreme until it was conquered and ultimately destroyed by the Internet). VCRs were popular back in the Dark Ages (the 1980s and 90s). They were in many homes and schools. Not only could you watch movies with a VCR, but you could even record TV shows and movies by using blank video cassettes. Supposedly, you could program a VCR to start recording a show or movie at a specific time, but only the most gifted in our society ever learned how to do this. For the rest of us, there was a little blinking light on the VCR that flashed "12:00" that served as a constant reminder to all who failed.

Now that we all know what a VCR is, let's return to class. At this point, the TV cart had been wheeled to the front of the class. The teacher would begin examining all the various electrical cords from behind the TV and VCR and they were plugged into the nearest wall outlet. Next, the TV was turned on. Phase 1 was now complete. Then came Phase 2 where the video cassette was successfully inserted into the VCR.

Before Phase 3 could start, the teacher would ask someone to turn off the lights. If your classroom was anything like mine was, there was never a shortage of volunteers of kids willing to turn off the lights. We were all pros at turning off lights. It was only when we were asked to come up to the blackboard and solve problems that we felt this wasn't part of our job description.

After the lights were turned off, the teacher would stand next to the TV with the remote in their hand and press the "Play" button. Phase 3 was now complete, and it was time to watch the film! Then suddenly, the unthinkable happened.

Nothing. The film wouldn't play. There was nothing on the TV but a blank screen. The class would begin to panic. Everyone had their hearts set on watching a film. Even the teacher was panic stricken because they hadn't prepared a lesson for the day and were counting on this film to get them to the finish line.

The teacher would ask someone to turn the lights back on, which was never as much fun as turning them off, by the way. After a few seconds of investigating, your whole class learned the terrible truth as to what had just happened: the film was last viewed by a horrible monster who hadn't bothered to rewind it.

You see, kids, back in the day, video cassettes were well-loved and cherished by those who possessed them, but with that possession came great responsibility. This included rewinding the video after you finished watching it. To not rewind a video was considered an unpardonable sin. Video rental stores didn't take too kindly to customers who returned movies without rewinding them. Some frequent offenders mysteriously vanished and were never heard from again.

So, now everyone had to wait for the teacher to rewind the film. The class period was only so long, and you knew as long as this film was being rewound, precious film viewing minutes were slipping away. Thankfully, moments later you would hear that beautiful "Click!"

sound that indicated the cassette was now successfully rewound and ready to watch.

Again, the lights were turned off, and the teacher proudly hit the "Play" button. The film was now ready to be watched ... or it would have been ready to be watched if the TV screen wasn't now filled with wavy lines in every direction and images that were jumpier than popcorn kernels in a microwave.

Yet again, the lights were brought back to the "On" position. By now, silent prayers were being sent to Heaven. It's likely some students were even praying to Saint Blockbuster, the patron saint of video rentals.

At this point, the teacher was on the verge of a breakdown. It was now necessary to undertake a ritual many users of VCRs had to perform called "tracking." This involved pressing or turning random buttons on the VCR and TV and praying God would show mercy. At this point, if you listened very closely, you thought you could hear your teacher mumble words under their breath that you didn't think teachers knew.

After fiddling with the VCR for awhile, if you were lucky, the teacher would finally figure out what the problem was. The problem was they didn't have any clue what they were doing so they got a student to show them which buttons to push.

With what precious time there was left, the teacher pressed the "Play" button one last time, and then it happened ... the fire alarm went off and everyone had to leave. As you were exiting the classroom, there was no doubt that this time you *definitely* heard your teacher using those same words you didn't think teachers knew.

Food: Congress should pass a law that within a block of any school there must be at least one unassuming hole-in-the-wall restaurant that serves great food at reasonable prices. When I was in high school, there was this great place down the street called Stadium Hot Dogs. We all called it "The Stadium." My little school unofficially claimed The Stadium as our own personal restaurant. Our mascot was the eagle, and if you ate at The Stadium, you were eating in eagle country.

The Stadium served specialty hot dogs, and they had a great selection to choose from. My personal favorite was what we called "The Pizza Dog." It was fantastic. When you bit into it, it was like eating a hot dog and a slice of pizza all at once. I don't know what magic or sorcery was used to create this edible creation, but I'm glad the chef used his powers for good instead of evil.

Sadly, while I was still in high school, The Stadium just didn't have the business it needed to stay afloat, and the owner decided to close. We learned the reason they had stayed in business as long as they had was because of the business our school gave them. Right before they closed, the folks at The Stadium gave each student in our high school a special good-bye present: one free specialty hot dog of our choice. Of course, I chose a pizza dog. I still remember eating that final pizza dog all these years later. I hated taking those last few bites because I knew

I wasn't just swallowing a hot dog, I was swallowing a precious memory.

Farewell, Stadium Hot Dogs. You will always have a special place in my heart and in my stomach.

Football: To be honest, football is my least favorite "F" word on this list. When I think about my experience with high school sports, I can think of a few other choice "F" words I can't really share in this book.

I went to the same school from the seventh grade until I graduated from high school. Our school had a flag football team, and if I recall correctly, every male student from these grades was automatically a member of the team. This meant I had to go to football practice as part of my P.E. Class. For most students, P.E. was short for Physical Education. For me, it was short for "Possibly Expiring."

I hated P.E. I hated running, I hated calisthenics, I hated trying to throw a football, and I especially hated trying to catch a football. Our principal, Mr. Strickland, was also the football coach, and he took sports very seriously. This meant we had to take sports seriously, too.

Back in school, Mr. Strickland would often tell us stories about former students. Some stories were funny, but other ones were stories where students had gotten into serious trouble. Sometimes I wonder if today, Mr. Strickland tells stories about me. If so, are they funny or serve more as a cautionary tale?

One story Mr. Strickland told us was one where a former student had gotten into trouble and ended up in his office. As Mr. Strickland counseled him, the student told him to his face something along the lines of, "You know, Mr. Strickland, I really don't care what you think." As you probably guessed, that was that student's last day at my school because Mr. Strickland sent him packing. I think it's safe to assume he didn't leave with a complimentary pizza dog, either.

When I first heard that story, I seriously considered waiting until my next football practice, walking up to Mr. Strickland while he was coaching, and saying to his face, "You know, Mr. Strickland, when it comes to football, I really don't care what you think." I didn't want to get expelled from school, just P.E. Thankfully, for the sake of my permanent record, I wisely chickened out. When a football was thrown in my direction, I just learned to duck and cover, a skill that has served me quite well throughout my life.

Fine Arts: While I was never very active in football, I was active in our school fine arts program. I loved performing in the school plays, and honestly, I wasn't that bad of an actor. The stage was my football field, and judging from the number of compliments I received after a performance, it was obvious I scored more than a few touchdowns of my own.

After high school, I didn't do much acting. I took one semester of acting at the local community college, but I didn't enjoy it. Taking an acting class at a community college is like being on an episode of *The Jerry Springer Show* but with slightly less regard for morality.

My favorite memories from high school were performing in our annual spring play. The school had grades from kindergarten all the way through twelfth grade. As was our custom, whenever we put on a play, the younger students were organized into a choir and provided the music and performed a small amount of speaking parts, but the majority of the acting cast came from our middle and high school classes.

Our Christian school always performed plays that explored various religious themes geared towards children and families. While some might not find this entertaining, trust me when I say we really had a lot of fun, even though we never performed the types of plays or musicals any of the local public schools would do for their spring productions. When you went to a school as conservative as mine, you knew you wouldn't be seeing a children's choir performing selections from *Les Miserables* or *Sweeney Todd*, though personally, I would have paid good money to see that.

Also, I should mention that while we always had lots of music and singing in our plays, we *never* had any dancing. This was a fundamentalist Baptist school, and dancing was a spiritual NO-NO. It was believed young people who engaged in dancing ended up committing assaults, robberies, and pulling down fire alarms and framing the Holy Spirit.

I'll never forget performing in the spring play during senior year. In junior year, our play had been canceled due to a conflict. This was to be our first play in two years, and would also be my last play before graduation. The theme of the play that year was something like "overcoming the giants in life." More on that later.

As was our custom, rehearsals began about a month before opening night, which was also closing night, because we always only had one performance. We viewed our plays the same way we viewed the Second Coming of Christ: it only happens once so don't miss it!

A couple of weeks into rehearsals, things were not going very well. Many of the cast were not memorizing their lines like they should. People were missing stage cues. It was one setback after another. Apparently, the "giants in life" were winning at the moment.

Finally, our director had enough. After an exceptionally bad rehearsal, we were all called up front to the stage and were told in no uncertain terms that if we didn't get our acts together, we wouldn't be acting at all.

After that, it was like our director had flipped a switch in all of us. It was now do or die. It had now become our mission to become a serious group of young actors. We buckled down, and almost immediately, rehearsals began to improve. Lines had been memorized. Scenes were coming together. There was an energy we hadn't felt before, but we were all feeling it now. We knew the play would be saved.

After weeks of rehearsing, the evening of the play finally arrived. We always performed our plays in the church across from our school building. The church was packed with parents, grandparents, aunts, uncles, you name it. The cast remained outside as the church filled up. We lined up and headed inside through a side door just offstage.

Soon, the play was underway. In previous years whenever I performed in our plays, I only had one role. This year, however, I had three separate roles. I played a modern day doctor in the first scene, Samuel from the Old Testament halfway through, and near the end, I played that always popular Biblical favorite: Goliath. When you only have so many cast members to go around, it makes things interesting.

Performing onstage was amazing, but for me, being offstage between scenes was just as amazing. It was like this nonstop adrenaline rush. By now, we all knew what was supposed to happen and when, and we had it down to an art form. Our "offstage" was the side room just off the stage where a small stairway led to the baptismal pool directly behind where the children's choir performed onstage. We had to make use of what little room we had. Had we tried to use the baptismal pool as our "offstage," it's possible some of the shorter cast members would have drowned between scenes.

When I was offstage, I had two separate costume changes between scenes. I was always fully clothed underneath and the costumes were made to fit over my clothes. We actually had a couple of female students assigned to help me change into costume and make sure my fake beards or whatever fake thing I was wearing at the time was on right.

I'm still amazed I was allowed to have female classmates help with the costume changes. In my high school, physical contact between members of the opposite sex was not highly encouraged. Several years earlier, our school play had two students play a husband and wife, and there was a hand-holding scene. There was talk, believe me. I guess, though, that the director knew if I didn't get help with my costumes, I would end up with my wig over my face and my beard between my legs so the powers that be consulted their King James Bibles and determined it was permissible under the circumstances.

The play moved quickly, and soon it was time for me to put on my last costume of the night and play Goliath. By far, I had more fun playing Goliath than any other part. I yelled at people and threatened various acts of violence. I know the school bullies in the audience were proud of me. It was rumored one or two of them even left that evening with tears in their eyes. Of course, Goliath died at the end, but many of my classmates seemed to enjoy watching me fall to the ground to my death. (This is just one of the many reasons why I choose not to attend reunions.)

Soon, the play had come to an end. The audience burst into applause. The play that almost never saw the light of day had ended up becoming one of the best plays to have ever been performed at our school.

As was our tradition, Mr. Strickland came on stage afterward and introduced each cast member. Everyone involved, no matter how large or how small their role was, got their moment in the sun. From the actors and singers to the sound crew and costume crew (who, by the way, had earned the nickname "Brandon's Babes," much to their disapproval), and to the director and the musicians, everyone had worked together as a team, and we had reaped the benefits of that teamwork. I only wish every moment of my time in high school could have been this amazing.

If I ever have a son, and my parenting skills are good enough that he lives long enough to make it to high school, I hope he follows in my footsteps and loves acting as much as I did. With my luck, though, he would be a natural born athlete and would rather play football than act. I already know this will lead to a heated argument and my shouting, "No son of mine is going to play football! You are going to be in the school play just like your father was! Now, you take this script and go up to your room and don't come out until you've learned how to enunciate your words like a real man!"

Friends and Fellow Classmates: Growing up, it wasn't easy for me to make friends, especially in high school. Because I'm legally blind, I was never really involved with sports. I also didn't have a driver's license, and still don't. At times, this made for some lonely days.

I was never without friends, though. These days, I've lost touch with most of my old high school friends, but two still remain. Their names are Allison and Sheila, twin sisters I actually first met in junior high. I first met Allison and Sheila back in the seventh grade. At the time, they were in the eighth grade. What can I say? I've always had a thing for older women. The day I first met them, my glasses had broken, and they came over to see if I was okay. Twenty-seven years later, they're still checking to make sure I'm okay.

Despite the fact we all still live in our hometown, the number of times I see Allison and Sheila in a year is about the same number of times I used to see them in an average week back in school. They both lead very busy lives. Allison and her husband work full-time and have a three-year-old son who keeps them on their toes. Sheila is single, but also works full-time. At the time I'm writing this book, she is writing a series of children's books that she hopes to publish in the coming months.

Like many twin sisters, Allison and Sheila have a very close bond. If, for example, Allison needs a break from being a mom for a few hours, she can call up Sheila, tell her what to wear, and then Sheila can come over wearing the exact same outfit. Sheila can then hang out with Allison's son for awhile and he probably won't be able to tell the difference. After nearly three decades, I still can't tell them apart at times.

Allison and Sheila are amazing ladies with so many God-given talents. They are both fantastic cooks, especially with making desserts. Allison makes some of the best homemade cupcakes you'll ever taste, and last year for my birthday, Sheila baked me this unbelievable cherry dessert that consisted of about ten percent cherries and ninety percent butter. When Sheila bakes you a dessert, you never have to worry about making room in the fridge for it. It'll be long gone before that ever becomes necessary.

In many ways, the three of us were in the same boat back in school. None of us was ever really popular. Our families didn't come from money. We led quiet lives and just tried to be good students and nice to those around us.

In one of our yearbooks, there is a picture with a few of the popular girls in Allison and Sheila's class at a school event. Allison and Sheila were in the picture when it was originally taken, but they were cut out of the photo by the time it made it to the yearbook. They were hurt by this, and it hurt me, too. If anything good comes from being left out, though, it helps us to know how bad it feels to be left out.

I'm not perfect. There were more than a few times growing up I could have been nicer to people. There were classmates who I could have asked to sit with me at lunch but didn't. There were others I could have invited to my birthday parties but didn't. Looking back, I couldn't really tell you why I acted the way I did at times, but I do regret it. As kids, we can be pretty stupid at times, but hopefully as we grow up, we learn from our past mistakes and become slightly less stupid adults.

With every book I've written, I have always found a way to include Allison and Sheila somewhere in each book. I've written stories about them and even dedicated books to them. They might have had their picture cut out of that old yearbook, but they have *never* been cut out of any of my books. As the years go by, I pray God allows the three of us to write many more chapters.

Feliz Navidad (Merry Christmas!): When you're a kid, December is an exciting month for two reasons: 1.) Christmas and 2.) Christmas Vacation! Two glorious weeks off from school! Since my parents were both educators, they also had the time off and were always able to stay home with me and keep me entertained the entire time. They were so excited about this prospect that more than once, I saw them crying tears of joy. Looking back, I seem to recall my teachers crying those same tears of joy on our first day back to class in January.

That last week of school before Christmas vacation was always sheer torture. I was always too excited to pay attention in class. I'm sure I wasn't alone. All the teacher ever wanted was just a few minutes of your undivided attention. A few of them might have even said those few minutes of undivided attention could even be your early Christmas gift to them. It never worked. The best gift they could ever hope to get out of you at this point was maybe a pencil sharpener shaped like an apple.

My mother worked in elementary education for years, and the number of Christmas gifts she received from her students that were "apple themed" was astonishing. No matter how tacky or cheap the gift was, if there was a picture of an apple anywhere on it, she probably received at least two or three of them. Years after her retirement, our house is still filled with "apple paraphernalia." We have more apple cups, apple bowls, apple candles, and apple shirts than we know what to do with. I remember my mom had a lot of rich kids in her class, and I always wished one of them would have gotten creative and given her a new Apple computer, but the closest we ever got was getting pencils that looked like worms to use in our own apple pencil sharpener.

I remember that last week of school before Christmas vacation always seemed to have some drama. I recall the time back in elementary school where my school was under attack by a mutant-like flu virus sent to destroy us all. My classmates were dropping like flies. They would come to school feeling fine, and hours later, they were lying in the hallway in the fetal position begging to be put out of their misery.

Somehow I managed not to get sick, and trust me, I was one of the fortunate ones. My poor teacher got sick, though, and even ended up with an exceptionally bad case of pneumonia. When we returned to school in January, we were treated to hearing her talk about it. Basically, the theme of the talk was "I Was Prepared to Die." After hearing her, so was I.

Remember the class Christmas parties? There always seemed to be an endless supply of Christmas cookies and brownies and cake and ice cream, not to mention every flavor of soda you could imagine. Usually the girls would stand around and discuss what gifts they had bought their family using their babysitting money. The boys usually stood around chugging soda in the hopes they would burp and the soda fizz would shoot up their nose. It was great practice for the office Christmas parties in years to come.

The class Christmas parties always seemed to have its drawbacks, however. I'm referring to the annual class gift exchange. I'm sure most of us did something like this back in school. Usually, you (or better yet, your parents) had to purchase a gift for you to give to one of your classmates. There was usually a price limit of no more than five or ten dollars.

Let's be honest. How many quality gifts can you really buy for five or ten dollars? There aren't many options. Had I ever had the chance to go on *$ale of the Century*, for five or ten dollars, I might have been able to buy a couple of bicycles or a camping package that I could have re-gifted, but I didn't have that option.

I remember one year at the class Christmas party the gift I gave to a classmate was a little toy racing car with a little race car driver action figure included. Honestly, it wasn't a bad gift. As a car freak, I would have been thrilled to get it. The classmate I ended up giving the gift to, however, made it very clear in no uncertain terms he was not impressed. I was crushed. Later that day when I got home, I burst into tears. He could have at least pretended to like the gift. I'm sure he probably never took it out of the package and perhaps gave it to someone else. If so, I hope the person he gave it to kept it in its original package and now it's worth a lot more than a few bucks. Somebody deserves some happiness from that gift. Heaven knows I never got any.

If anything good came from that experience, I learned a valuable lesson about being gracious. I learned that while you may not always like the gift you're given, you should still be grateful and sincerely thank the person for their gift, unless of course, they gave you that flu virus that was going around, but that goes without saying.

I had to put this belief into practice a few years later. Even in high school, we still had Christmas parties and gift exchanges. One year, the classmate who drew my name gave me a paperback book. I remember the title was *The Pathfinder*. At the time, I thought a book was a lousy gift. Today, I love reading so much so that when I die, I hope to be buried next to the local Barnes & Noble.

When I first received this book, I remembered how I had been treated at that earlier gift exchange. I didn't want to do to this classmate what had previously been done to me. I thanked him for his kind gift and told him

I looked forward to reading it. It was one of the greatest performances ever in my young acting career.

Believe it or not, even though I now love to read, I still have never read *The Pathfinder*. When I first brought the book home after the Christmas party, I tossed it aside and eventually realized I had misplaced it. As time went by, I just forgot about it. A few years ago, I was cleaning out my attic and found it stuffed in a box with a bunch of other books and papers. I was really excited and quickly set it aside with the plans of finally reading it and … then I misplaced it again and still haven't found it.

If the former classmate who gave me *The Pathfinder* happens to be reading this, I truly am thankful for your gift. I'm sorry it took me years to realize it. Also, do you happen to know if they ever did a sequel to *The Pathfinder* called *The Bookfinder*? If so, if you could please send me a copy of that book, I would be even more truly thankful.

This last Christmas-themed story is a personal favorite. It takes place when I was in the seventh grade, just before our Christmas break. One day, a classmate of mine rode to school on his brother's new bicycle. When he arrived at school, he chained the bike to a nearby telephone pole and went about his day. That afternoon, he accepted a ride home from someone and decided to leave his brother's bike chained to the pole all night. This would prove to be an unwise decision.

The neighborhood where our school was located wasn't in the best part of town. Crime wasn't uncommon. When my classmate returned to school the following morning, he learned this the hard way. When he went to check on his brother's bike at the telephone pole, he made the terrible discovery that the chain was still there, but the bike had been stolen. I'm amazed the chain hadn't been stolen, too. To be honest, I'm sort of amazed the telephone pole hadn't been stolen.

This story could have ended here, but thankfully, it didn't. I don't know whose idea it was to begin with, but the decision was made to raise money to buy a new bike for our classmate's brother. Students volunteered to ask around school for donations. I can't recall how much money was collected, but through the kindness of my classmates and the generosity of a local department store, my school was able to purchase a new bike to replace the stolen one so my classmate's brother would have it in time for Christmas. I think we all experienced the Christmas spirit that December day.

Sadly, I wasn't able to contribute to the bike fund. I wanted to, but on the day they collected money, I wasn't carrying a wallet and had no money on me. I didn't even have any spare change. To this day, I still kick myself that I couldn't help.

Through this experience, I learned a couple of valuable lessons. First, you should always be willing to help those in need. Second, you should always be *able* to help those in need. Since then, I make a point to carry my wallet and have a couple of extra dollars on hand in case something comes up. You never know when you'll need a little extra money for yourself, or just as important, for someone else who may need it.

F- for Kindness: When you're young, you do things you're not proud of, and I'm no exception. I chose to write the following story in the hopes someone reading this will learn from my mistakes.

When I was in high school, I had a classmate, who, for privacy reasons, we'll call "J." When J first came to our school, three things became quickly obvious. First, he wasn't a very good student. In his previous schools, J had fallen through the cracks and never got the help he needed to succeed academically. The second thing that was obvious was J had a severe weight problem. He didn't even use the same kind of chairs the rest of us used. He had to use a much larger, stronger chair to support his weight.

The last thing that became quickly obvious was that despite J's struggle with school and his weight, he was one of the nicest people you would ever want to meet. J loved people. He loved to smile. He was the type of guy who accepted you no matter what. Some students, myself included, felt like they were not welcome in certain social cliques, but that didn't seem to deter J. He had the courage to just sit down with whomever he wanted to and just start a conversation. I wish I had that kind of courage, then and now.

J remained at our school for several years. During that time, many wonderful things happened in his life. J became a Christian. One of the older students led him to the Lord one day in a classroom. J loved Jesus.

J also became a better student. Our principal, Mr. Strickland, was a wonderful and patient man. We were a small Christian school, and J was now where he could get the personal attention he needed. Mr. Strickland worked one-on-one with him, and he improved academically.

Despite his improvement in school, J always struggled with his weight. The impression I got from J was that he wasn't really concerned, and I think many of us assumed all was well. We were wrong.

It happened during our last break of the day. Many of us were outside hanging out and talking, including J. He was sitting at one of the old wooden picnic tables we had outside our building. Unfortunately, J chose to sit right in the middle of the bench at its weakest point. This bench was old and worn and couldn't support his weight. In a matter of seconds, it broke in two and J fell to the ground.

What did we do? Did we help J up? Did we make sure he wasn't hurt? Nope. We laughed. We laughed hard. That's what we did. I laughed harder than most. We thought it was funny. To our defense, we thought J thought it was funny too. Mr Strickland soon heard the commotion and came over to investigate. What he saw wasn't funny to him at all. He made sure J was okay. Mr. Strickland did what we should have done, but didn't.

The next day, J wasn't in school. It turns out he had been hurt by breaking that bench, but it wasn't the kind of hurt you could see with the eyes. We got a well-deserved lecture from Mr. Strickland about how words and actions can harm others. We never meant to hurt J. We thought we were laughing with him. It turns out we were laughing *at* him.

Thankfully, J was back in school the next day. To be honest, I couldn't really tell you if I apologized to him for laughing. I seem to recall saying I'm sorry, but I couldn't tell you for sure. If I did, it was a haphazard apology at best. Teenage boys have a difficult time grasping the concept of "I'm sorry." We made the collective decision to put this incident behind us. J seemed to know we were sorry, and that's what mattered.

In the coming months, J made a difficult decision. Despite all the improvements he had made in school, he still struggled. There was no way he would graduate on time, and J knew it. We all knew it. J decided to leave school and go to work. I had heard someone in J's family had offered him a construction job where he could make decent money.

I don't remember having the chance to say goodbye to J. I remember he was there one day and gone the next. Mr. Strickland later shared J's decision with the rest of us. He told us he gave J a goodbye hug. There were no hard feelings. J did what he had to do.

I saw J a few months later when he came to school for a surprise visit. We were glad to see him. We talked for a couple of minutes and soon, we said our goodbyes, and I left to do something else. Little did I know this would be the last time I would ever see J. We lost touch after that. I thought about him through the years, but I never made any effort to reach out to him. Life goes on.

Back in 2011, I learned the terrible news. I was informed J had passed away at the age of twenty-nine. A friend had emailed and told me she had run into another one of our former classmates at J's funeral. She assumed I knew J had died, but I hadn't heard.

J left behind a family. He left behind a child. I had heard J still struggled with his weight, but I don't know for sure. If so, I couldn't tell you if his weight played a role in his death. What I can tell you is J is truly missed by those of us who were privileged to know him.

When I think about J, I think about all the love and joy he brought to our lives. In my mind, though, I keep coming back to that day back in school when he fell to the ground and all I did was laugh. If I could relive that moment, things would be much different. Offering a hand is so much better than pointing a finger.

Rest in peace, J.

* * *

Fast Forward: A lot has happened in the twenty plus years since high school. Over the last two decades, my former classmates and I have experienced many college graduations, marriages, divorces, births, deaths, awards won, jobs gained, jobs lost, weight lost, and weight gained. Sadly, for some of us that includes hair losses, too.

Right after graduation, Mr. Strickland, along with members of his family who also worked at the school, resigned from their positions and left to establish a new church and Christian school. When I first heard the news, I wasn't completely surprised. The last couple of years had been difficult for Mr. Strickland. I could tell he was growing discouraged, but I never really knew why. He even admitted to us that he had considered resigning on more than one occasion. We knew that the pastor of the church our school was affiliated with had been making decisions that many students disagreed with, and Mr. Strickland and his family had, on more than one occasion, gotten caught in the crossfire.

The situation continued to deteriorate, and the time had now come for Mr. Strickland and his family to take a major leap of faith. The church and school they founded has now completed its twentieth year in ministry and continues to go strong. Our former high school, however, didn't fare as well. The last time I checked, they had a new pastor and principal, but only about a third of the students it once had.

In the summer of 2018, Mr. Strickland celebrated his seventieth birthday. In the months leading up to his birthday, many of his former students, myself included, received a group message on Facebook from Mr. Strickland's daughter, who was also one of my former teachers. She and her family were planning a big seventieth surprise birthday party for Mr. Strickland, and they wanted to invite his former students and their families to the event. Each student who was planning to attend was asked to prepare something along the lines of an 8.5" x 11" scrapbook page with the student's family name, a family photo, an old picture from their school days, and a written portion where we were asked to share a special memory of Mr. Strickland. When I first read this, I was like, "Wow! Is this for a grade? Does neatness count?"

I continued reading on. The message also said they were planning to present Mr. Strickland with a special plaque to acknowledge his work with our football program. If anyone deserved a plaque it was Mr. Strickland. He loved our football team and took pride in serving as our coach. I knew it would be a special day.

Because of my issues with large crowds, I made the difficult decision not to attend Mr. Strickland's celebration. Regardless, I knew I still wanted to do something special for him. I wanted Mr. Strickland to know how grateful I was for everything he had done for me. I decided to write him a letter and mail it so he would receive it just after the celebration/reunion was over. I didn't want to risk sending it too early and ruin the surprise.

What you are about to read is the letter I sent to Mr. Strickland. I left out a sentence or two and changed a few words for privacy reasons, but it's still from the heart. I hope reading this letter will encourage others to reach out to their former teachers and principals and tell them how much they meant to them. Those educators who have made so many sacrifices to teach us need to know just how much of a difference they have made in our lives. Here is my letter:

Dear Mr. Strickland,

I wanted to take a few moments to write you and wish you a Happy (Belated) 70th birthday! I'm sorry I missed your celebration the other day. I knew there was going to be a large crowd, which is wonderful, but not necessarily for those of us who are <u>very</u> claustrophobic.

However, I didn't want this milestone to pass without taking a moment to tell you how much you have meant to me. Looking back, I don't think I could have asked for a more wonderful principal. You have been one of the finest examples of a Godly, Christian man I have ever known.

Thank you for the wonderful chapel messages you brought us every week, along with your daily devotions. Thank you for never being ashamed to share your faith in Christ, and for your desire to encourage us to do the same. I will never forget the day back in 1995 where we knelt in your office and I asked Jesus to come into my heart and save my soul. That is the best decision I ever made.

Thank you for all your hard work in the sports program. While you always wanted a victory, you taught us the importance of being both a humble winner and just as important, being a humble loser. I'm sorry if I hurt you by not participating much in the sports program, including not attending many of the football and basketball games. What I'm about to write is not intended to hurt you in any way, but I just felt many of my classmates valued sports a little too much. Because I wasn't good at sports, I often felt they didn't really value me. It was very hard for me to attend those games, and I never really had much peace when I was there.

Despite what you may have thought at times, though, school pride was important to me. I tried to show that in the activities I did excel at, like choir and the school plays. These were some of the BEST memories I have from my time at school! I know you weren't as involved in those areas, but your family was very much involved, and you always set a great example for them to follow in how they led our rehearsals and directed our plays.

There are so many more great memories to share, like all the great stories you told us after morning devotions. Thank you so much for allowing us to try to sidetrack you in our daily attempt to start class time roughly two minutes before our morning break.

Thanks for all the time you spent helping us with our school work. Physical Science still haunts me to this very day! Also, thanks for trying to let me be the final student to ever complete my typing course using the electric typewriter, and for eventually giving up hope I would ever finish and letting me switch over to the computer.

Typing is one of the best skills I ever learned in school. I've self-published four Christian humor books. I never sold too many copies of any book, but God used those books in some amazing ways, including raising funds for children's charities and mission projects in my church.

Thanks for taking the time to read this letter. I pray God's continued blessings on you and your family. I wish things had worked out that you could have remained at our school, but I understand why that didn't happen. Thanks for staying long enough to help me graduate (on time). I know if I had been a year younger, though, I would have gone over to your new school with you. I would have been just as proud to graduate as a Lion as I was to graduate as an Eagle.

May God continue to bless you with many more wonderful years on this Earth and many more birthday celebrations to come and many more young people to love.

Sincerely,

Brandon Boswell
Proud member of the Class of 1999

$$* \quad * \quad *$$

Final Thoughts: When thinking about our pasts, some cherish those times while others don't. Like a lot of people, I'm somewhere in the middle. I choose not to live in the past because of the bad memories, but I still try to hold onto the good ones.

My schooldays left me with a lot of memories. Looking back, I wish more of my classmates had taken the time to get to know me, and truth be told, I wish I had taken more time to get to know many of them. I wish we all could have focused more on the things we had in common and not cared so much about all our differences. Who knows how many lifelong friendships there could have been. Regardless, we can't go back to the past. We can only reflect on it and, hopefully, learn from it.

One final "F" that I've learned from my schooldays is forgiveness. I've learned that when we hurt one another, we must learn to forgive. When we don't forgive, we fail, and if school taught us anything, failure is the one "F" we can all do without.

Class dismissed.

THE FAMILY REUNION

Recently, my mother's side of the family held a reunion. Since my mother was one of the organizers, it was pretty much a given I would be attending. Her goal was to have as many of our relatives attend no matter what it took for them to get there, be it by plane, car, train, boat, or bobsled. In regards to traveling by bobsled, though, I don't believe we have any relatives that far north. We're a proud Southern family. If we travel past Richmond, we feel we've reached the point of no return.

After weeks of preparation, the day of the reunion finally arrived. My mother wanted us there about two hours early to get ready, which meant I would be waking up two hours earlier than I normally would or wanted to on a Saturday morning. If getting out of bed at seven in the morning on a Saturday isn't a sin, it should be. After breakfast, we packed up the car and were on our way.

The reunion was held at my aunt's home out in the country, about an hour from our home in the city. As we drove, Mom continued her role as organizer and looked through her notebook of names and numbers, trying to make her last minute preparations. When we got to my aunt's, she wanted to set up a display of old family photographs. Mom had brought many of her own and phoned her cousin from the car and asked if she could bring some of her old photos, too. It was her goal to have the largest display of photos of long dead relatives I knew nothing about as she possibly could.

We finally arrived to the little rural community where the reunion was to be held. Before going to my aunt's house, we stopped at the little Methodist church a mile or so away. Both my mother and father grew up in this area. They attended this church as children and teenagers. They were married there in 1965. Their parents, my grandparents, are all buried in the small cemetery behind the church.

Before the reunion, my mother wanted to change the flowers on her and dad's parents' graves. We drove past the church and the fellowship hall and parked at the entrance to the cemetery. My parents got out of the car and walked over to the graves with the new flowers.

As they worked to change the flowers, I watched them from the backseat. After a few moments, I had to look away. Watching them reminded me the day will come when my parents will no longer be there, and my older sister and I will be the ones standing in that same cemetery putting flowers on their graves. A few minutes later, they finished up and returned to the car. We drove away, and I didn't look back. I was just grateful to have left the cemetery with both my parents alive and well.

Several minutes later, we arrived at my aunt's home. For years, she has lived in an older two story home on a large plot of land on the Intracoastal Waterway. She had been preparing for this reunion for weeks, if not longer. Everything was clean and tidy. Dirt had *not* received an invitation to this party.

We unpacked the car with the plastic plates, utensils, and napkins. I had never seen so many napkins in my life. My parents bought them in bulk, and you would have thought we had the messiest family in the world. We came to the conclusion that years from now after we're all dead and gone, our descendants will still be using this same box of napkins for their reunions.

Soon, my mother and my aunt were putting the pictures and decorations in their designated places. I stayed out of the way the entire time. I learned a long time ago to just let women put what they want where they want it, and where they usually want me is out of sight. I chose the safety of a comfortable chair on my aunt's screened-in back porch overlooking the water.

My mom and aunt discussed taking pictures. Mom suggested taking group photos on my aunt's pier. My aunt felt this wasn't a good idea because some of the boards were loose and she didn't want to take any chances. A lot of work had been put into this day and she didn't want it to end with a story on the local news that started with "A family reunion turned tragic today … "

Soon, the relatives started to arrive. Hands were shook, hugs were given, and conversations were now underway. At this point, I had three choices. I could:

A. Make an effort to walk over to everyone and start engaging others in conversation.

B. Make an effort and walk over to everyone and just smile and give the impression I'm engaging others in conversation.

C. Let others approach me as I continued to sit in my comfortable chair on my aunt's porch letting the breeze hit me in the face as I watched yachts and sailboats travel up and down the waterway.

Well, as I learned back in school, when it comes to multiple choice questions, when in doubt, pick "C," so I stayed on the porch. Make no mistake, though, I was still part of the action. Whenever anybody came up with a casserole dish in their hands to put inside the house, I held the door open for them. By doing this, I helped to ensure that the person holding the dish didn't drop it before entering the house, thus ensuring we would be able to consume the contents of the dish.

I am a hero.

Also, whenever anyone wanted to get out of the sun and rest for a few minutes, they just came up to the porch to sit down and I kept them company. I like one-on-one conversations better than trying to talk to five people at once. I was able to meet one elderly relative who was the daughter of my mom's Aunt Bessie. I was told this lady was the spitting image of her. I never knew Aunt Bessie, but at least now I know what she looked like.

Soon, it was time for lunch. My mother was chosen to say the blessing and soon after, we took our places in the food line. The boyfriend of one of my cousins barbecued a pig and other relatives brought smaller side dishes. Country people are the best cooks in the world and there is nothing anybody can say to make me think otherwise.

Everyone chose to eat inside, but since crowds in enclosed spaces make me nervous, my family was fine with me eating outside. I loaded up my plate with barbecue and extras and headed back to my seat on the back porch to continue watching the boats as they passed by.

Sometimes when a boat rode close to shore, I waved to those on board. I had hoped someone would see me and wave back and possibly mistake me for the person who lived in this house. Gas station attendants such as myself don't often get the opportunity to be mistaken for waterfront homeowners.

As I sat on the porch, I just enjoyed the day. With every bite of barbecue or potato salad or biscuit, I was reminded that food always seems to taste a little better when you're eating it near the water.

One of my relatives had prepared this great carrot souffle dish I couldn't get enough of. I love it when people are blessed with the God-given talent of turning vegetables into desserts. It brought back memories of when I was growing up, and after church on Sunday, my parents and I would ride over to the cafeteria in our local mall for lunch. They served this amazing carrot souffle. I would have eaten multiple portions had they let me. They say carrots are good for your eyes, and if that's true, my goal was to walk into that cafeteria legally blind and leave with 20/20 vision.

Thinking about the carrot souffle made me recall this wonderful waitress who worked in the cafeteria at the time. I never knew her name or anything else about her, but whenever I saw her there, she was always busy working. She was a quiet lady, but she always had a positive attitude and made sure her customers always had what they needed.

The cafeteria closed years ago, and I always wondered whatever happened to that waitress. I wonder how she is and what she is doing these days. Wherever she is, I hope she's happy. It's funny how a little thing like carrot souffle can trigger a fond memory.

* * *

As the day wore on, I spent as much time on that porch as I could. It was so peaceful there. As I looked out over the water, I was reminded how life on the coast had been such a big part of my family's heritage.

Decades earlier when my parents lived here as kids, they played in this same waterway. They went swimming and water skiing and loved it. I can't imagine my parents as kids themselves, nor can I ever imagine them on water skis. They were a lot braver than I would have been. If I were to ever attempt to step on a pair of water skis, with my luck, I would actually be stepping on a couple of water moccasins cleverly disguised as water skis.

My grandparents loved living on the coast, especially my mother's parents. My grandfather, who we called Granddaddy North, worked as the local bridge tender on a draw bridge that has long since been torn down and replaced with a high rise bridge.

Granddaddy North had a wonderful sense of humor. I would like to think I inherited his sense of humor. I was always told he could do hilarious impressions of people he knew. I know I didn't inherit *that* from him. For the last eleven years at my job, I've been trying to do an impression of someone who knows what they're doing, but my bosses never seem to buy it.

North was a whiz at math. He was so good with crunching numbers that when the first calculators were available in the stores, he bought one just to make sure the calculator was working correctly.

North also loved the outdoors. If he wasn't working on the bridge, you were likely to find him either gardening or fishing. He loved fishing. My mother once told me he was such a devoted fisherman that when a lightning storm came up, my grandfather wouldn't pack up and go home, he would just continue fishing in the thunder and lightning by putting a metal washtub over his head for protection. It's a miracle my grandfather survived those fishing trips. I only wished he could have survived his heart attack.

It was in February of 1984. North was working on his car, a 1971 Ford LTD sedan. My grandfather loved Fords. It was the only car brand he bought. His dream was to buy a new Ford Thunderbird. He had test driven one, but hadn't bought it yet, and sadly, never would.

As he was working on the car, he started to feel sick and went inside the house to rest. It was the beginning of the end. Two days later, he had died of a massive heart attack. My mother said it was like his heart exploded. Planning his funeral was the most difficult thing she ever had to do. Granddaddy North touched a lot of lives. That fatal heart attack left many of our hearts permanently damaged as well.

My grandmother, who we all called Granny, started to have serious health issues soon after North's death. My family wanted Granny to move in with us. My parents even had a bedroom and bathroom built onto our house for her, but Granny refused to leave her home. She had lived in that house since the Thirties and wasn't about to leave. For better or worse, she lived there for another fifteen years, just down the road from the site of the former drawbridge where my grandfather had worked for so long.

Granny was an amazing cook. She had the golden touch. She could preserve figs with the same care and attention as a historian preserving an antebellum mansion. Granny made amazing cakes. If she had trouble sleeping, she would get up early and bake. She loved making cakes for people. She even made cakes for her doctor that she would give him when she had her appointments. It was like Granny's own unique health insurance policy. As long as she fed her doctor, in her mind, he would do whatever it took to keep her alive for as long as possible.

Growing up, my parents and I would drive up and see Granny every other Friday afternoon and spend the night. When we got there, Granny would have supper waiting. My favorite meal was her homemade hash. She knew just how to cut up the meat and potatoes just right. She also made incredible handmade biscuits. If we were really lucky, there might be some homemade fudge or sweet potato pudding for dessert.

After dinner, we would all adjourn to the living room and watch a little television. Remember now, Friday night was TGIF night on ABC and that couldn't be missed. After the last comedy of the night was over, I would take a shower and soon, it was time for bed. Granny had several bedrooms and most of the time, I got to sleep in an old queen size bed in the largest room. When I was a child, that bed felt so huge and I felt so safe. On cold nights, Granny or my mother might come in and give me an extra blanket. Sometimes there might be a thunderstorm during the night. Granny's house had a metal roof and the sound the rain made on that roof could give any ASMR video a run for its money.

On Saturday mornings, we would wake up and Granny would fix breakfast. She usually made oatmeal, which normally wouldn't be most kids' idea of a fun breakfast, but Granny always poured just the right amount of brown sugar in it to ensure I maintained just the right level of hyperactivity before my Saturday morning cartoons. Looking back, this might explain why cartoons always seemed funnier at Granny's house.

Later that morning, Mom would drive Granny into the nearest town so she could do her grocery shopping, pick up her prescriptions, and God willing, buy some fish and shrimp for our dinner before we headed home. My grandmother loved seafood. Her philosophy was that the best food is born wet and dies fried.

After Mom and Granny returned from town, my father and I would get in the car and make a quick trip down the road to visit with his parents. My other grandparents, who we called Grand Mommy and Pop, lived in an old house out in the woods. I loved them very much, but I *hated* going to their house. Snakes lived in those woods, and from time to time, one would slither its sorry self into their house. Pop wasn't fazed by this, though. If he saw a snake, he would just grab his hoe and chop it up. I, however, would have frozen in fear, thus making it so much easier for the snake to chop *me* up.

I can't recall ever sleeping over at Grand Mommy and Pop's house. Even as a little kid, I didn't want to be in that house overnight. I feared that I would go to sleep clutching my favorite stuffed animal and wake up the next day to discover I was cuddling with a cottonmouth. For whatever reason, I never really worried about snakes at Granny's house. She had open fields all around her house, so I always figured if I could see the snakes coming, I could get a running start.

What I did worry about at Granny's house, though, were field mice. Every so often, one would find its way into her house. She would set out traps, but that didn't always stop them from getting inside. I always had this horrible fear that one night we would be sleeping over and I would get up in the middle of the night to go to the bathroom and end up stepping on a field mouse with my bare feet in the dark. Had this scenario occurred, I'm quite certain I would have ended up putting a head-shaped hole through that metal roof I loved so dearly. Thankfully, I never had a mouse sighting.

While I never saw a field mouse at Granny's, I saw plenty of dogs – lots of dogs. Granny never really liked dogs, but they liked her. The neighborhood dogs knew how good of a cook she was, and they knew where to get the best table scraps for miles around. I'm just as nervous around dogs as I am field mice or snakes, and since I didn't want to be mistaken for any of those table scraps, I usually stayed indoors.

Looking back, I actually did spend a lot of time indoors at Granny's. Every room was fun in its own special way. In one of Granny's bedrooms stood an old upright piano that I used to love just pounding on all the keys. When I got bored with the piano, I often found myself in Granny's living room sitting on the floor and drawing by using an old step stool as a makeshift desk. Many hours of my childhood were spent on that floor creating artistic masterpieces worthy of display on our nation's finest refrigerators.

I often played out on Granny's screened-in porch where she kept her rocking chairs and her washer and dryer. It was fun rocking as I watched cars drive by on the nearby road. Sometimes I would play with my Matchbox cars and line them up on the windows in the porch or better yet, I would race them up and down the porch. I played more than a few games of "Chicken" and "Demolition Derby" with those cars. Had I kept them in better shape, I could have made up for all the money I lost when my parents threw out my *Ghostbuster's* slime.

I remember once when I was eight, Granny's washing machine leaked. When I walked out onto the porch, I had discovered I now had my very own indoor swimming pool. In my eight-year-old mind, this was the coolest thing ever. Granny and my parents were in the middle of a panic attack, however, and were trying to find anything they could to soak up the water. I, on the other hand, was trying to find whatever object I could so I could play my new favorite game – "Will It Float?"

As the years went by, the time eventually came that Granny was unable to live on her own anymore. At first, my mother tried finding someone to stay with her, at least part-time, but nothing really worked out. Granny could be very demanding. Anyone she tried to get either wasn't good enough, or if they were good enough, something came up and they couldn't continue doing the job. In the last few months of her life, my family made the painful decision to have Granny live in a nursing home a few miles from our home so she could be closer to us.

I can recall the one time I went into Granny's house after she had been moved out. By then, a number of items from her house had either been put in Granny's new room at the nursing home or had been given to other relatives. It was a somber experience. I remember walking into her living room and seeing an empty space on the wall above her couch where a picture of a beach scene had hung for years. I walked into her bedroom and the hospital bed my parents had gotten for her was now gone. For the first time in sixty years in that bedroom, no bed stood, for we knew Granny would never spend another night there. With Granny now gone, there was no life left in that old house. I remember walking out of the house for the last time. I wanted to stay, but I was so glad to be leaving.

I remember visiting Granny in the nursing home. I remember standing outside the door of her shared bedroom as I listened to her cry to my mother that she wanted to go home. I remember her trying her best to comfort Granny as best she could, but knowing this was now her home, for better or worse.

Granny was never happy in the nursing home. We had hoped she would get used to it in time, and perhaps even make a few new friends, but that never happened. It didn't help that Granny also was in and out of the hospital, and we found out at that time she had been having an allergic reaction to one of her medications.

Granny was miserable. My family was miserable. She wanted my mother there with her constantly, which was impossible since my mother was working full-time. She would come home exhausted from work, but soon it was time to visit Granny at the nursing home. For the next six months, it was a constant juggling act in my home with all of us, especially for Mom, who was being pushed in all directions.

In December of 1999, just two days after Christmas, my family and I were at home when we received a phone call from the nursing home. Granny wasn't doing well, so my parents went over there to see what they could do. I didn't go. I was tired. I was frustrated. I loved Granny, but I loved my mother, too, and I was tired of seeing her so exhausted and frustrated all of the time. While my parents were gone, I sat in my bedroom and prayed. I remember talking to God and saying out loud, "God, Mom can't take much more of this." It was a prayer prayed out of anger and desperation.

Later that day, my parents returned home. As they walked through the front door, Mom was crying. She came over, hugged me, and said, "She didn't make it." Granny had been taken to the hospital where she died of congestive heart failure at the age of eighty-seven. Mom had said earlier that day when they got to her room, Granny had said, "Well, I'm dead." My mother, always trying to reassure, told her, "Mama, you're not dead." Granny knew it was time, though. I never asked her what her final words to Granny were, or if she got to tell her everything she wanted to before she passed. Some things are best left private.

I never told anyone about the prayer I prayed that day, but in my mind, I kept coming back to it and the guilt I felt for praying it. Grief will do strange things to you. I know now that my prayer had nothing to do with her death. It was Granny's time, and God was calling her home. I guess the angels in Heaven were getting pretty hungry by now and wanted some of her homemade hash and biscuits with a side of fudge and sweet potato pudding for dessert.

The funeral was held a couple of days later at the little Methodist church just down the road from Granny's old home. It was very well-attended. I had hoped she would live long enough to see the year 2000, but Granny didn't like change, so she just decided to leave this world in the century she liked best. Granny touched a lot of lives in her eighty-seven years on this Earth. Granny wasn't always the easiest person to get to know, but you always knew where you stood with her. Regardless, she loved God, her family and her little community, and led her life as best she could while cooking some great meals along the way. Even if Granny didn't like you that much, you still might be lucky and get a piece of homemade pie or cake from her. It was always best to stay on Granny's good side, though, because if she did like you, your piece of pie or cake would be just a little bit bigger.

* * *

As I sat watching the water, I took a few moments to think about my late Uncle Malcolm, my mom's brother and Granny's son. I never knew Uncle Malcolm very well, even though he and my aunt lived just a couple miles from Granny.

Malcolm was a private man. He bravely served his country in multiple tours of duty in Vietnam, and I'm certain he never fully got over the images he saw over there. I overheard my mother talking once and she said that the only time she ever heard Malcolm discuss Vietnam was when he had commented on the number of body bags he saw over there. She knew not to press him for further details.

Malcolm was a good man, though, and loved my aunt and his three daughters very much. I remember when I was a kid, he had given me this poster of a mint-green first-generation Ford Thunderbird. That picture hung in my bedroom for years.

I remember the day of Uncle Malcolm's passing. It was in mid-December of 2005. He had gone into his local hospital for an operation. Mom couldn't be with him because at the time, she was battling cancer and undergoing chemo and radiation treatments. That afternoon, we received an email that the operation had gone very well and they hoped Malcolm would be able to go home very soon. At six that evening, we received a phone call from a family member that Malcolm had died suddenly. He was back in his hospital room and they were trying to get him into a chair when he just slumped over and never woke up. At the time, I was home alone with my mother. It was now my turn to try to comfort her in much the same way she had tried to comfort her mother. I did the best I could, but I knew my best would never be good enough.

As I continued to watch the water, I thought of the family that remained but could not be here on this day. I thought about my elderly cousin Louise. She and her husband Al had lived up the coast in a little fishing community called Atlantic, the same place where Granny was born and raised. Al was a school principal and Louise taught school for many years in Florida. They had held on to her old family home in Atlantic and eventually moved back there after they retired. They never had any children of their own, but their students were their children.

Louise was always faithful about remembering the birthdays of the kids in the family, including my own.

Whenever she would send a birthday card, she would not only include a little money in the card, but whatever age you were turning is how much money she would send. If you turned nine, she gave you nine dollars, ten dollars for turning ten, and so on. Even as a kid, I had hoped this would be a tradition that Louise would carry on until I reached middle age, but no such luck.

I remembered attending a surprise ninetieth birthday party for Louise a few years ago. It was actually the last time I had seen some of the same relatives I was now seeing at the reunion. The party was held in the fellowship hall of the Methodist church she attended in Atlantic. I had been there once before for Louise and Al's fiftieth wedding anniversary years earlier. Al and Louise remained married for sixty years, but he died shortly after their last anniversary.

It was a stormy day in early January, and as we traveled to the party, I watched out the car window as dark clouds filled the sky and the choppy waves crashed on the shore alongside the road. I remember after the party was underway how warm and safe it felt to be in that fellowship hall with Louise and surrounded by family. The room had been decorated with old school desks and schoolbooks like Louise would have used from her time teaching all those decades earlier. If Louise were still teaching, I'm quite certain whoever had done the decorating would have gotten a well deserved A+.

Sadly, Louise is now in a nursing home, and according to family members, she doesn't recognize the relatives who have gone to visit her in recent months. Even at the party years earlier, I could tell her memory was fading, but she still was basically aware of who we were and where she was. More importantly, she was aware of how much love there was for her.

* * *

The day wore on, and within a few hours, the reunion was coming to an end as people started to leave. We packed up our car with leftovers my aunt was gracious enough to give us, so we wouldn't have to worry about cooking for the foreseeable future. We said our goodbyes and left just as a thunderstorm rolled through. We traveled down those winding country roads in the rain, mostly in silence because my mother wanted to sleep, or "rest her eyes" as she calls it. Looking back, I think she just wanted some quiet time to reflect on the day's events. It was now time for her "back porch" moment.

We didn't stop and ride past either of my grandparents' old homes. My father's old home place was sold after my grandparents passed away. We learned there had been a fire in the house years earlier and it was completely destroyed. A new more-modern house now stands in its place.

Granny's house was also sold. The person who bought it first was a cousin. He told my parents once that sometimes when he was in the house, out of nowhere, he would start smelling the aroma of food cooking in the kitchen but when he looked, there was no one there. I guess if Granny couldn't be there to cook anymore, at least her memory could still linger like the smell of fresh made biscuits cooling on her kitchen counter.

My cousin eventually moved out of the house, and I believe it has been on the market on more than one occasion. It's just too sad for my mom to return to the house where she grew up. We had been informed at the reunion that a large amount of land in the area had been sold, and we were told it included Granny's old house. There were plans to redevelop the area and turn it into a large RV park. Whether or not this happens remains to be seen, but so help me, if they tear down Granny's house, I hope whoever is living in those RV's is never haunted by the smell of good country cooking. They don't deserve such an honor.

As we got closer to the city, we made several stops at dollar stores to pick up several items we needed. I selected several items I wanted to purchase but didn't feel like waiting in line, so I pulled out my wallet and gave my father the money and returned to the car to sit with mom. He returned a few minutes later and told me that I had change, but he had donated it to a literacy program the store was collecting money for. This annoyed me because I wanted my change back. The first thing I thought was *Okay, fine, but as soon as they learn to read, the first book they better buy is one I wrote.* The more I thought about it, though, I began instead to think, *God, thank you blessing me with a father who is still alive to annoy me.*

Two days later, Mom informed me she needed to see the doctor for a skin issue. Since my father drives me to work, I would need to leave about an hour earlier so we could get her to her doctor's appointment. At first, that same annoyance sank in, but it was soon quickly followed by the thought: *God, thank you for blessing me with a mother who is still alive to inconvenience me.*

Family reunions can be bittersweet. Not only are you reunited with your family, but you also reunite with your past. You cherish the time you have with your loved ones in the present, but fear what the future holds after they are gone. You recall the funerals of those you loved and look forward to the weddings of other loved ones and the births of their children destined hopefully to become your loved ones as well. May we pray those children will grow up to take time from their busy schedules to come together and remember us after we leave this Earth and are finally reunited with our loved ones for our eternal reunion.

TALES FROM THE GAS STATION AND BEYOND

Whenever I announce to friends at work I'm writing a new book, they get very excited, far more excited than me, actually. All they have to do is read the book. They get the easy part. I, however, have to write the book first, and that's not so easy. What is easy, though, is knowing what my readers have come to expect. In the case of my coworkers, they expect funny stories about our experiences working in retail.

I've worked in retail for eleven years, with nine of those years as a gas station attendant. When you work in retail, often times, you feel like you're never as well-trained as you should be. Sometimes you feel like you've been thrown to the wolves. You only hope the wolves received even worse training than you did and don't know how to do their jobs, either. When I was in graduate school, the first course I ever took was Improvisational

Comedy. I honestly believe that the skills I learned in that Improv class have helped me more than any on the job training I've ever had. Knowing how to crack a joke has helped me diffuse some difficult situations, even though at times my comedic timing was what originally caused the difficult situation.

Working in retail isn't easy. Working a retail job outdoors can be even worse. For example, when I'm walking around the gas station, usually with my trusty hand-held grabber picking up all the litter that blows around the area, I have to worry about stepping in fire ant hills. My coworkers inside the main store don't have to worry about stepping in fire ant hills. They have to worry about stepping in a lot of other things, if you know what I mean, but not fire ant hills.

Fire ants are horrible. You leave work one night and everything is fine. You return the next day to find a little mound of dirt that wasn't there yesterday. Those of us who have any experience with fire ants know we're looking at a newly formed fire ant hill. We also know that if fire ant killer isn't sprayed on the hill immediately, the ants will quickly spread. That lone little fire ant hill will likely turn into two fire ant hills, then three, then, who knows? Soon, you're dealing with a fire ant neighborhood. At this point, the fire ants will likely form a homeowners' association and you will have to go through them to get approval to spray. Like many homeowners' associations, they are very unlikely to grant your request. If you work outdoors and you go to the higher-ups and tell them about the ant hills and their response is along the lines of "Try not to step in them," then you just have to learn to try to coexist peacefully and watch your step.

Fire ant hills aren't the only thing I have to worry about stepping in when I'm picking up litter. (You're probably thinking if I didn't pick up so much litter I wouldn't have to worry about stepping in stuff, but I can't help it. I grew up watching a lot of cartoons in the Nineties and *Captain Planet and the Planeteers* made me fear that if I didn't pick up litter, there could be dire consequences.)

Anyway, when I'm picking up litter, I also have to worry about stepping in dog, uh, "droppings." On more than a few occasions, people choose to walk their furry friends around the gas station and the surrounding area. I'm fine with this, because I think dogs are cute, but NOT when they are dropping "atomic bombs."

Here's how this frightening scenario usually goes down. I'm walking around with my grabber, picking up candy wrappers and thinking to myself, *Yep. This is exactly why I went to grad school.* Suddenly, I start to smell something in the distance that doesn't smell too good. I go to investigate because I fear what I'm smelling could be a possible gas leak. (In a way, I guess it sort of is.) I walk to where the source of the smell is, and if I'm not careful, I know I'll be stepping in what can only be described as "memories of meals gone by." My only hope is that if I do step in "it," right afterwards, I accidentally step in a fire ant hill. Those ants wouldn't know what hit 'em, and that should at least take care of our ant problem.

* * *

Let's talk about the daily struggle of working with managers. I wanted to include this in its own section because transitioning from dealing with fire ants and dog poop to dealing with your boss doesn't always make for the smoothest transition.

When dealing with managers, I often wonder if they are really listening to my concerns. I have my doubts. At the time I'm writing this, there has been a light on my gas station canopy that has been flashing for months now. Basically it's like my own personal strobe light. Sometimes when there aren't any customers around, I like to stand under it and pretend like I'm singing along at a Grateful Dead concert.

Of course, I go to the higher-ups and tell them about the light, so now, the waiting game can officially begin. Days turn into weeks, and still the light continues to flash, almost as if it's mocking me. I return to the higher-ups and ask for an update. I'm told there has been a work order put in to fix the light. I begin to wonder how they went about putting in this work order. Did they call or email or text the necessary department to report the light? Perhaps. From the amount of time I've been waiting, however, I'm beginning to wonder if instead they found a turtle walking by the store, strapped a post-it note on the outside of its shell with a brief description of the problem, pointed it in the direction of whatever different state or country our company's Facilities Maintenance Department may be located, wished it "Godspeed," and sent it on its merry way. Until that fateful day when the light is finally fixed, I continue to make the most of the situation. I keep apologizing to all the annoyed customers, and in keeping with the Grateful Dead ambiance I've grown accustomed to, I strive to memorize the lyrics to "Truckin," a very "gas station appropriate" song, I might add.

Of course, we have to talk about the weather when we talk about working outdoors. Working outdoors is great when it's bright and sunny and there's a nice breeze with a high of seventy-four and a low of seventy-three.

This, however, isn't always the case. If you work outdoors year round, you learn to quickly adapt to changing weather conditions. You learn to deal with working in below-freezing temperatures with heavy winds or working in the extreme heat with no wind whatsoever. Working in the wind is like dealing with a visit from your extended family. When you have it there and you want it, it's great. If it's there and you don't want it, you think it will *never* leave. Throw in some heavy rain, and you have all the necessary ingredients for a heaping helping of human misery.

I remember one particular shift at the gas station. It hadn't been a particularly good day. The gas prices had gone up and, as it always goes, the customers continued to let me know they weren't happy about it. Apparently, I had left my magic gas price changing wand at home that day so I couldn't wave it and knock that extra penny a gallon off unleaded. I was getting *very* frustrated.

Remember earlier when I wrote about all the different scary story themes out there? Well, this includes Scary Gas Station Stories. I've heard more than a few stories where a customer attacked the gas station attendant. I don't recall ever hearing one, though, where the gas station attendant attacked a customer. I was about one more complaint away from changing all that. Since I didn't want to be the lead character in any Scary Prison Stories, however, I held back.

As the day wore on, the sky began to change. The sun was now covered by large ominous clouds. Over the next few minutes, the sky grew increasingly darker. Then, the rain started. Soon, the wind started to pick up. I knew I was about to become an unwilling victim of a Southern phenomenon we call the Pop Up Tropical Storm.

In the back of the gas station we keep our large gas price signs. Suddenly, a strong gust of wind sent both signs moving. Since they were on stands, it was like watching a foot race. Personally, I was rooting for Diesel. As I watched the signs try to blow away, I kept thinking it was bad enough the customers leave when the prices go up, but you know it's really bad when the prices themselves try to make a break for it.

So, of course, by now I'm totally soaked. My lunch break couldn't start fast enough. I walked into the main store to eat and hopefully dry off. The wind and rain continued pouring down in buckets. It was so strong even the lights in the store flickered on and off. I thought a blackout could occur at anytime. Knowing this, I made a point to ride the elevator up to the break room instead of taking the stairs because in weather conditions like these, it's far better to get indefinitely stuck in a dry elevator than being definitely stuck out at a wet gas station. Sadly, the elevator made it all the way upstairs without any problem. I only hoped that when it came time to ride it back downstairs after lunch, my luck would change.

* * *

The following pages contain some of my favorite work-related stories that I experienced first-hand or were first-hand accounts told to me by coworkers who presumably think they could ever top any of my stories. Here, for your reading pleasure, are some of our personal favorites from the employee break room:

Show and Don't Tell: I think we've all experienced something similar to this first story. Not long ago, I had an encounter with a customer at the gas station who drove a large expensive looking SUV. His gas tank was on the driver's side and he didn't want to wait in the longer line with the other vehicles that had tanks on the same side as his vehicle. Since our gas pumps can be used from both sides, I politely suggested he could drive to a pump that wasn't being used on the other side and just bring the nozzle around his vehicle and just fill up his tank that way. Quite a few customers do it, and as long as you show a little common sense in how you do it, it can be done safely. His response, however, was that he was *not* going to do that on an $80,000 SUV.

Now, if he doesn't want to do this, that's his right and I respect that. What I don't respect is when he felt obligated to share with me how much money he presumably paid for his SUV. To me, this behavior is about as rude as it gets. I've even had close friends who do this. I really don't want to know how much you paid for your car or your house and most importantly, I *really* don't want to know how much money you make at your job. On behalf of all us who feel this way, please stop sharing every intimate detail of your financial lives with us. If you can't stop, though, at the very least, could you start buying us much nicer birthday and Christmas gifts? You really have no excuse anymore now that we know you can afford it.

If You Can't Say Anything Nice, Then At Least My Page Count Still Goes Up: This next story was told to me by a coworker who works in Carts. He was a young man who, at the time of this story, hadn't been out of high school that long. Like a lot of people in his age group, most likely this retail job was helping him earn money for his higher education.

So, sometime ago he was pushing a line of shopping carts from one location to another. As he was working, he was noticed by a young child and an older woman, presumably the child's grandmother. My friend said he overheard the two talking. The child had said to the woman something along the lines of, "Why is he pushing all those shopping carts?" The older woman's response was along the lines of, "Because he didn't get good enough grades in school."

Now, I may be wrong, but I seem to recall this particular friend telling me once that he graduated from high school with honors. Now, I may be wrong yet again, but I seem to also recall him telling me that before that woman and child left the store that day, she learned first-hand he had indeed graduated from high school with honors.

Words can hurt, and we all need to be careful what we say around others. The moral of this story: Always assume everyone graduated from high school with honors; otherwise, everyone may assume you got kicked out of finishing school under not-so-honorable circumstances.

$$* \quad * \quad *$$

Life In The Fast Lane; Death In The Driveway?: From the moment I first heard this story, I knew before I left this Earth I would not only put it in my next book, but I might even write the next book for the sole purpose of including this story.

Another coworker, who also worked in Carts, told me about the time he was helping a female customer load groceries into her vehicle. As he was helping her, he noticed how fresh the car smelled and how spotlessly clean it was. For a man to notice such details is pretty huge.

My coworker, being a nice guy, commented to the lady how great he thought her car looked and smelled. The woman's response was along the lines of, "Thank you. My husband actually died in this car."

If I recall correctly, my friend's response to this was along the lines of, "Uh … what?"

My response would have been, "Well, I think you can finish loading these groceries by yourself. See ya."

Honestly, I really don't know what to write at this point. I'm sure there are some good jokes out there, but would any of them really be appropriate? I will say, though, that when her husband died, I sincerely hope he was in the passenger seat. I would hate to think anyone would die alone in their car. If he did die alone, however, I hope he at least had the voice on his GPS to keep him company on that fateful day. That's better than nothing, unless of course as he was leaving this life for his final eternal destination, the last voice he heard was, "You are going the wrong way. Turn around."

I truly hope the car this man died in was one he really wanted to buy and had all the options he wanted in a vehicle. Cars are very important to us men. Women have "bucket" lists. We, however, have "bucket seat" lists.

* * *

Don't Let the Door Greeter Hit You On The Way Out!: Retail is a difficult line of work to be in. The pay isn't great, the hours are long, and then, there are the customers, the "necessary evil" of the retail world.

To be fair, my co-workers and I have some wonderful customers who we absolutely love. Seeing them is sometimes the best part of our days. We work hard to serve them, and in return, they often give us handshakes and hugs.

Then there are the bad customers who quickly become the worst part of our days. We still work hard to serve them, but all they ever seem to give us is a hard time. Some of these people are so mean-spirited that if we tried to shake their hand, we fear that they might put a hand grenade in our hand and just walk out. I'm not certain if our company policy would allow us to throw the grenade back at them. Of course, if we did throw it back, we could say truthfully we're not allowed to accept gifts and gratuities so we had to give it back.

When you work in retail long enough, the bad customers can *really* get to you. Once at the gas station, I had a customer who drove up to a gas pump. I politely asked the person to pull up to the front pump so the car behind them wouldn't have to drive around theirs. They not so politely refused. Then the customer spent, in my opinion, far too much time at the gas pump talking to their friends who had come in another vehicle. Next, instead of leaving like I so desperately wanted this person to do, they walked over to me and wanted to buy a soda out of a cooler we keep at the station to raise money for charity. This person started digging through the ice to find just the right drink. They just *had* to have a certain kind. One of my regular customers happened to be filling up their tank at the time, and she was standing next to the cooler. She politely suggested this person try a certain soda, but instead of thanking her for the suggestion, this customer spoke coldly toward her and said they didn't want *that* brand. Finally they found the soda they wanted, which we were selling for one dollar apiece. Instead of giving me a dollar, however, this customer handed me a one <u>hundred</u> dollar bill that they wanted me to break. I told them truthfully I couldn't make change for a bill that large, and they ended up putting the drink back, which actually made me feel a little better. I would have felt a *lot* better if I could have instead replied, "Okay, that'll be one dollar for the soda, and can I assume the other ninety-nine bucks is my tip for having to put up with you for the last ten minutes?" Of course, I couldn't say that. Thankfully the customer drove off shortly after, and I haven't had any contact with this person since. (Oh, where are the hand grenades when you really need 'em?)

As you have probably guessed by now, those of us who work in retail often fantasize about how we would like to deal with our rudest customers. I'm talking about the ones who are just asking, no, *begging*, to be taken down a peg or twelve. Sadly, that pesky fear of unemployment and financial ruin often keeps us from saying what we really want to these people. We learned a long time ago that we just have to be professionals and take it. That's not to say there isn't the occasional victory, however.

In my store, our Door Greeters are not only a great source for the latest gossip, but also great comedy material. Not long ago, I was walking back out to the gas station from my lunch break and I ran into one of my Door Greeter friends. I could tell from how excited she was I was about to hear a great story. She proceeded to tell me about a customer she encountered a few days earlier. There was a problem with his purchase or something, so she politely instructed him to speak to a nearby cashier for assistance. This man apparently did *not* want to speak to a nearby cashier for assistance.

According to my friend, the situation got very tense. He was starting to raise his voice at her. Finally, he asked to speak to a specific manager. For the purpose of this story, we'll call this manager "Sam." The man, now visibly angry with my Door Greeter friend, said to her, "I want to speak to Sam!" My friend stood her ground and in a firm voice told him truthfully, "Well, Sam doesn't work here anymore." This customer must not have been as close to Sam as he thought because Sam had transferred to another one of our stores weeks earlier and apparently had not disclosed this information to this man. When the customer realized Sam couldn't help him, it was like he knew he had been defeated. This guy's one lifeline in the store had been removed and he was on his own. Well, not totally on his own. He still got to speak to the nearest cashier for assistance.

My Door Greeter friend was proud that day. She stood her ground and came out on top. She said later that day, that same customer walked past her on his way out and didn't even look at her, most likely out of embarrassment. If he had, he would have seen her with her head held just a little higher that day. Some might say the moral of this story is "It's not what you know, it's WHO you know," but I say the moral is, "Before you start making a scene, make sure WHO you know hasn't taken a job in South Carolina."

* * *

Wrong Way, Right Lesson: Over the years, I've made my share of mistakes while working as a gas station attendant. Granted, I've yet to blow anything or any*one* up, but still, I have regrets. The following story is one such example.

One busy Saturday, I was working at the gas station. Traffic was heavy, and on days like this, customers don't like waiting in line. Because the station is designed to have cars enter from a specific location and exit from a specific location, however, sometimes people have to wait patiently.

On this day, a lady in a sedan tried coming in from the wrong direction. I was standing close to where she was trying to drive into, so I got her attention and firmly told her she couldn't enter the station from that direction. From the time she opened her mouth, I personally felt like she was getting defensive with me. This made me stand my ground and dig my heels in further. Eventually, she did turn her vehicle around.

I was frustrated. Like I've done on so many other occasions, I started complaining to the other customers about having to deal with this lady. I said to one random man, "Can you BELIEVE her?!" I recall saying something else about her to him, but can't remember what. I know it wasn't very flattering.

It was at this time I learned a valuable lesson. If you're going to complain about one random customer to another random customer, make sure the random customer you are complaining to isn't MARRIED to the random customer you are complaining about.

Yep, of all the customers in the gas station, I ended up complaining to this woman's *husband* about her as he was filling up *his* vehicle. Needless to say, he wasn't happy about this and made it abundantly clear to me.

I had messed up BIG TIME. I'm not going to lie. I really didn't want to get in trouble with my manager. Whether I got in trouble or not, though, I knew what I needed to do.

By now, the man's wife was waiting off to the side of the station while her husband finished pumping his gas. I walked up to her driver's side window and began talking to her. I apologized to her for my actions. Yes, she shouldn't have tried driving into the station from the wrong direction and yes, I did have the right to say something to her about it and I believe she understood this now, but I still didn't act like the professional I claim to be. Worse yet, I didn't act like the Christian I claim to be. Thankfully, she graciously accepted my apology and we talked for a few more minutes. She actually turned out to be a very nice lady. After they left, I actually did call my boss and told him what happened. Telling the truth can be hard, but it still has to be done. Thankfully, just like this woman, my boss turned out to be pretty understanding.

I'm not sure if this couple have ever returned to the gas station since that day. I always wonder, though, when I was apologizing to her, if I had said to her about her husband, "Can you BELIEVE him!?," would she have gotten just as mad, or, perhaps just maybe, have said, "Tell me about it!"

$$* \quad * \quad *$$

Eyes Up Front, Ears Listening, Engines Off: Not long ago, the customers and employees at a gas station in my hometown had a rather frightening experience. Somehow, a customer's car caught on fire at the gas pumps. Soon after, an explosion occurred. By the grace of God, there were no injuries that I heard of, but two cars burned, at least two gas pumps suffered severe damage, and the underside of their canopy suffered extreme smoke damage. Since this gas station is just down the road from the one where I work, this was just a little too close for comfort.

This incident became quite the news story around town. People wanted to know how the fire started. One rumor was that the car that caught fire had its engine running while the owner was pumping gas and this ignited the fire, though I couldn't tell you if this is true. In case you didn't know, having your engine running while pumping gas is what we in the fuel industry call a Class A "No-No." If you choose to do so, the results could potentially blow up in your face … and everywhere else, so please don't do it.

A few days later, I was at work, hanging out in the break room with a couple of friends, Victoria and Tina. They asked me what I would do if a fire ever broke out at our gas station. I said to them, "You see these two long things sticking out below my waist? They're called 'legs.' In the event of a fire, I will be using them to carry me as far away from the flames as humanly possible." Judging from their reactions, I think it's safe to assume they agreed with my exit strategy.

Speaking of exits, I think it's about time we exit this chapter. Don't worry, though. My coworkers and I will be back in the next chapter, and this time, we're spicing things up with a major hurricane that could destroy us all! Stay tuned!

FLORENCE

In September of 2019, those of us lucky enough to call Eastern North Carolina home had to contend with a rather unwelcome visitor by the name of Hurricane Dorian. In September of 2018, we had to deal with an even more unwelcome guest by the name of Hurricane Florence. September can be a rough month here in the coastal region. It reminds me of that old song by Green Day, "Wake Me Up When September Ends." Personally, I'd rather be awakened by the end of August so I can be sure to be on an extended bus tour of Nebraska by the first of September.

Hurricane Dorian devastated the Bahamas as a Category 5 storm, but thankfully, by the time it arrived here in ENC it skirted the coast as a much weaker Category 2 storm. As Dorian was coming close, a lot of us in ENC were like "Hey! Day off from work. Some rain. Some wind. Let's have a hurricane party!" As Florence was coming close a year earlier, however, the storm was a strong Category 4 for quite sometime and the collective mindset around here was more like, "Dear Jesus, please forgive us for our sins."

Let's talk about preparing for a strong hurricane. If I were to ask you what are some supplies you would need during a hurricane, what would you say? Bread? Yep. Milk? You bet. Non-perishable canned goods? Of course. Batteries? Oh yeah. A large box of Moon Pies and multiple bottles of Pepsi? Sure. In the South, it's the law.

What if I said, "How about gasoline?" You would be like, "Well, of course you need gasoline! You always need plenty of gasoline for a hurricane! You need gas for your car if you evacuate and you need gas to power your generator if you stay and you don't have power for a few days." Then you would probably say, "Brandon, you're a gas station attendant, how could you ask such a question?" Then, at this point if logic has finally kicked in, you might ask, "Brandon, were you working at the gas station the week the storm hit?" I would then say, "Yep." Then, if you were to ask, "Was it a bad week?" I would then say, "YEP." (Any "yep" where all the letters are capitalized is rarely a good "yep.")

Working at the gas station the week Hurricane Florence was projected to hit us was probably about as life-threatening as the hurricane itself. It was like being a military of one. I knew I was on the front line and about to embark on the mother of all battles.

If you think ISIS or Al-Qaeda fighters are terrifying, they're nothing compared to the terror of having to reason with an eighty-year-old grandmother in a Cadillac with all her cat figurines wrapped up in a beach towel in her back seat trying to fill up her tank so she can make it to higher ground who decides at that very moment, "Hey, there's only about ten cars waiting behind me in line, this would be the perfect time to wash my windows." Even as I approach, I know the enemy has already won.

I'm not going to write much about working at the gas station that week. I'm still trying to repress the memories. (It's like the field trip to the medical lab multiplied by infinity.) Thankfully, I wasn't scheduled to work on the last day the station was open before the storm. I was told it closed early, and the customers who had been waiting in line who were turned away did not find the humor in the situation. I'm quite certain had I been working that day I would ultimately have ended up as the lead character in a Scary Grim Reaper Story.

Since I wasn't scheduled to work, I stayed home and helped my father board up our front windows and bring in the rocking chairs off the front porch. Only welcomed guests get to use the rocking chairs, and Florence wasn't welcome. We were hoping she would take the hint and move on.

My family didn't know if we would remain at home or evacuate. We packed our travel bags just in case. My father and I threw what we could into a bag without really thinking. For my mother and sister, this process took considerably longer because they had to select just the right wardrobe. Apparently they weren't certain if fleeing for your life from a hurricane is considered a formal or informal occasion.

After days of preparation, Florence finally made landfall late on a Thursday evening. By the grace of God, the storm had been downgraded from a Category 4 to a Category 2 by the time it came ashore. Unfortunately, Florence was a slow moving storm that stuck around for approximately two days. It's weird how you can find yourself in a situation where you're holding your breath and breathing a sigh of relief all at once.

Within the first few hours of the storm, we lost power. Thankfully we had a generator, but we had to be careful to preserve our fuel. We were also without cable and Internet. For much of that time, I stayed in my bedroom upstairs and read whatever books I could find while avoiding having any more contact with my family downstairs as was necessary. I love my family, but I learned a long time ago that when I'm confined at home with my loved ones for an indefinite period of time, I need to spend as much time by myself as I can so they can remain my loved ones.

Sitting alone in my bedroom listening to the wind and rain outside my window was quite enjoyable, actually. A lot of my time was spent in my old leather recliner rereading some of my favorite Garrison Keillor *Lake Wobegon* novels and revisiting some of my favorite characters from the fictional Minnesota town. It even gave me a possible story idea for a new book: a Lutheran pastor from a small

Minnesota town leaves the ministry and moves to Los Angeles to become a private investigator. He uses the skills he learned while in the Lutheran church to solve various crimes. The working title I had was "Sex, Lies, and Lutefisk." I talked myself out of the idea, though, and honestly, I think the world is better off for it.

When I wasn't reading, I was just rocking away in my recliner and just thinking. I thought a lot about my coworkers. I wondered how they were doing during the storm. I prayed for them and their safety. I was really starting to miss them. It's funny how you can be at work and your coworkers can get on your nerves and all you can think about is going home and being with your family. Then, after being stuck with your family for a couple of days, all you can think about is how desperately you want to be with your coworkers at that moment. You even begin to wonder if any of them have a spare room they would like to rent out when the storm is over.

It's funny how people deal with stress. For all my fears and phobias, hurricanes don't really bother me. In fact, I find them exciting. My sister, on the other hand, seems to be always afraid we're all going to die, so she's really not the most pleasant person to be around during a hurricane.

During the storm, from time to time, I would get hungry and come out of hiding long enough to mosey on down to the kitchen to partake of a Moon Pie. I had to be quiet, though, because I didn't want my sister to catch me. If she did catch me eating one, she would freak out. She was like, "Why are you eating all the Moon Pies? We need those! We don't know how long we'll be trapped here! If you eat all of them, we could starve to death!" To appease her, I would usually put the Moon Pie back in the box and spend the rest of the day unsure of when I could get my next Moon Pie fix. In the South, Moon Pie Deficiency is a very real health concern. I think I read an article about it on WebMD, or maybe it was Wikipedia. I'm not sure. It was somewhere on the Internet so I know it's real.

By Saturday, Hurricane Florence was finally winding down. It looked like we were all going to be okay. We were still alive with Moon Pies to spare, I might add. For safety reasons, our church had previously canceled services for that Sunday. That afternoon, my father and I decided to get out of the house for awhile. As is our family tradition, after any hurricane, we ride around with our ancient camera we bought new around 1993 and take pictures of the storm damage.

Before we pulled out of our driveway, we surveyed the damage around our home. We had already had a bad leak in my bedroom that caused me to lose sleep during the storm and quite a few shingles had blown off our roof. We knew the police didn't want people driving around town, so we just drove around our neighborhood. As we rode around, we were in awe of how much damage there was. Streets were covered with debris of all shapes and sizes. Numerous trees had fallen and had taken power lines down with them. Many roofs that had once had shingles now had blue tarps covering them.

When the cable and Internet were finally restored days later, we were able to get our first look at the storm damage throughout the area. It was breathtaking for all the wrong reasons. Large portions of towns in the surrounding counties had been flooded. Homes and businesses were underwater. Roads were impassable. Those same blue tarps covering roofs of damaged homes in our area could now be seen throughout the region. Many homes were now unlivable, but at least the homeowners were alive to pick up the pieces. Some weren't so fortunate. Those of us who lived through Florence knew there would be many challenges in the days, weeks, and even months ahead. Only time would tell what the final outcome would be.

* * *

It's been over a year since Hurricane Florence struck Eastern North Carolina. For many of us, things have returned to normal. Others, however, still continue to struggle. While many homes and businesses have been repaired, many others still sit abandoned.

Everyone who lived through Florence has a story to tell. Some stories are powerful and dramatic. Some survivors can give detailed accounts of rescuing their neighbors who were caught in the floodwaters, either as trained emergency responders or just Good Samaritans trying to help those in need. Many survivors can share emotional stories of having to live indefinitely in storm shelters and not knowing when, or if, they would be able to return to their homes. There are many stories of people volunteering weeks of their time to give aid and comfort to storm victims, even as they were victims themselves. You couldn't help but be touched, and perhaps a little convicted, by all the stories of people who invited their friends and neighbors to stay with them until their homes could be rebuilt.

Hurricane Florence taught us many important lessons. What I learned might be different from what others learned, but we can all learn from each other. Here are the lessons I learned from Hurricane Florence:

Radio Disc Jockeys Make Pretty Good Preachers: During and shortly after Hurricane Florence, watching TV and going online were not options for many of us. Many landline phones also went down, and at times, some of us couldn't even get cellphone reception. If we wanted to know what was going on in the outside world, many of us had one choice: the radio. This often meant having to get information passed on to us by many of the local radio disc jockeys.

Now, if the disc jockeys where you live are anything like the ones in my area, on any given normal day, some of what they say and do on the air can be pretty over the top. It's pretty clear that for more than a few disc jockeys, strong ratings and strong morals don't always go hand in hand.

After Florence, however, our local disc jockeys were incredible. Many of them stayed on the air for many, many hours each day to broadcast what information they had about the hurricane recovery. I'm certain they sacrificed a good bit of sleep, hot meals, and hot showers during this time. Disc jockeys from rock and roll stations partnered with others from country stations and pop music stations to broadcast live together from the same studio so their broadcast could be listened to simultaneously on multiple stations.

As phone lines continued to be restored, listeners were able to call in from all over the region and share what was going on in their community. Through the work of these disc jockeys, we learned about road conditions, shelter openings, relief efforts, and the like. They knew this wasn't a time for ratings; it was a time for survival. It was a time to help their neighbors, and they encouraged their listeners to do what they could do to help those in need like bringing a meal or bottled water to someone or opening our homes to others to let them take a hot shower. I could tell these radio personalities really cared about the needs of others and put those needs before their own.

During the aftermath of Florence, many local disc jockeys became "preachers" in their own right and had given their listeners some of the best radio "sermons" we needed to hear during this difficult time. It just goes to show you that God can use anybody for good who is willing to help, and that includes me, you, and even "Bubba and The Crew from the Mornin' Zoo."

* * *

Help Me To Help You: If you have never been through a hurricane, trust me when I say that recovery can take a *very* long time. It can be days before any sense of normalcy returns. And, if you think it is dangerous working at a gas station the week before a hurricane, believe me when I tell you it's nothing compared to working in a gas station the week *after* a hurricane. Thankfully, my store had implemented what we were calling "disaster hours" and we weren't required to come in and work our scheduled shifts because we were in a state of emergency. We could come to work if we wanted to, but I didn't want to because I knew people were even more panic stricken by now, and honestly, I wanted to live long enough to publish this book.

Being at a gas station after a hurricane is beyond scary. I had coworkers who covered my shifts who told me horror stories that even Stephen King would find unbelievable. The hurricane had knocked out many of the gas pumps and those that were working still had issues. People were impatient. My coworkers were in disbelief. I found out later one customer even tried to cut in line in his car and it almost ended up in a fistfight.

I'm sorry, but I don't get paid combat pay, and breaking up fistfights isn't part of my job description. That's why God created managers. If a fight is going to happen, it's going to happen without me. As the old adage goes "There are no atheists in foxholes and there are no martyrs in gas stations."

Don't get me wrong. If I witness someone trying to cut in line and they get beat up for it and now they're lying in a pool of their own blood, I'll do something. First, I'll call them an ambulance. Then, as we're waiting for the ambulance to arrive, I would ask them questions to help them stay alert such as, "What's your name?" or "What's your street address?" or "Were you born this stupid or did you take courses?" After the ambulance arrived and they're being put into it, I would then offer my last words of comfort, which I hope would be, "Don't worry about moving your car. While you were slipping in and out of consciousness, the other customers doused it with gasoline and set it on fire and pushed the remains into the first empty parking space they could find." (Now *that's* what I call a truly polite customer.)

* * *

Helping one another is important, especially after something terrible like a hurricane. There are many ways to help, but some ways are better than others. In the case of my choosing not to work at the gas station right after the hurricane, some might argue I wasn't willing to help. I argue that I did help by realizing I wasn't the best person to help at the time. An anxiety-prone, legally blind gas station attendant may get the job done on a normal day, but perhaps not right after a natural disaster. At the time, people who could see a little better, think a little clearer, and stay a little calmer were needed. I gladly stepped aside so I could live a little longer.

Sometimes when we try to help, we end up doing more harm than good. What's the point in helping those in need if after you help them they're in even more need? After Florence, many people had major damage to their homes, and good workers were needed to help repair the damage and make their homes livable again. Since I have absolutely no experience whatsoever in construction, I feel I have no business offering to help repair homes. If your home wasn't condemned before, it would be by the time I crawled down off the ladder, that is if I could make it down the ladder without falling on my face. I can't really help others when I'm lying in a hospital bed and you can't really help others if you have to take time out of your day to drive me to the hospital because every ambulance in town is too busy responding to the gas stations where people cut in line.

Throughout my life, I've heard more than a few football analogies about being a good team player and knowing when to get in the game. Sometimes, though, being a good team player means knowing when to leave the game and sit on the bench for awhile and let others take the field. Some people are better suited to score touchdowns, whereas others may be better suited to carry water to the other players or carry the first-aid kit when another player is injured. It doesn't mean you're any less a part of the team, but you may be better suited at serving in a different role.

When I'm trying to figure out how to help someone in need, I pray and ask God to point me in the right direction. This was certainly the case right after Florence. I needed to know how to best help, and prayer has often been my first step in that process.

As a result of my prayers, God led me to help people I knew personally, specifically my coworkers. To help me figure out who needed help the most help and what kind of help they needed, I began talking to coworkers. I asked questions and paid close attention to what they were saying.

I won't lie. This was rough. I learned a lot of coworkers suffered a wide variety of damage in the storm. Some people were lucky and had minimal damage such as siding blown off their houses or a few leaks in their roofs. Others, however, had trees fall through their roofs and suffered major damage. One coworker not only lost her home in the storm, but her mother *and* grandmother also lost their homes, too. Just hearing these stories left me feeling overwhelmed. I couldn't even begin to imagine how overwhelmed the people were who were living through this nightmare.

After I determined who needed the most help, I decided the best thing to do was reach out to my coworkers with cash donations or purchase gift cards for them to use for groceries or toiletries or whatever they needed. (When you can use a gift card in a store you already work at, it makes life a little easier.)

Working in retail as long as I have, I've never gotten rich, but I was taught the value of saving your money for a rainy day, or just as important, saving your money to help others during their rainy days. Sadly, in this case, many of my coworkers had been caught in the rain without an umbrella.

For the next couple of weeks, I surprised unsuspecting coworkers with cash donations and gift cards. The looks on their faces were priceless. It felt good knowing I had done my small part to help the people I not only work with, but also care about as well. I didn't spend a lot of money, and looking back, I know I could have done more. Still, I like to think in my own small way I made life a little easier for others. Sometimes giving someone a little more peace of mind can be the best gift you can give.

Many of my coworkers had the same idea. I learned that one lady I worked with had taken in stray animals to care for who were without a home during and after the storm. Others donated linens and other toiletries to storm victims, along with many, many other acts of generosity and kindness. It goes to show you don't have to make a lot of money to still make a difference.

* * *

Hurricane Florence was a terrible storm that served as a good reminder about true giving. Helping others often means making personal sacrifices. It means being willing to give up on our wants at times to meet the needs of others. This could mean giving others our time, talents, and of course, our material possessions. No matter how we help, may we thank God for the opportunity to help those in need and continue to trust in Him as our shelter during the storm and strive to be His rainbow to others after the storm.

LET'S REVIEW! (CONCLUSION)

Many months ago, I began the process of writing this book and now here I am, sitting at the computer getting ready to write out the conclusion. Writing a good conclusion is like trying to say a heartfelt goodbye. I've never been very good at saying heartfelt goodbyes. From the amount of time I've spent staring at the computer screen, apparently I'm not very good at writing heartfelt goodbyes, either.

When I started this book project, I knew I wanted the conclusion to be something special. My goal was to write something so brilliant that anyone who read it would say, "Wow! That was so thought-provoking!" The closest I can seem to get, though, is, "Wow! What was he thinking?"

Throughout the writing of this book, I used my previous books as references numerous times, so I thought once more couldn't hurt. I skimmed through the pages of those books one last time to see if it would spark any ideas on how to end this one.

A lot has changed in my writing and in my life since writing my first book back in 2001. Despite those changes, I discovered that the conclusions I came to at the end of each book were always pretty similar.

First, don't just believe in God, actively seek God. He loves you. You might not think you deserve to be loved. I think we've all felt that way at one time or another. Thankfully, God loves us despite everything we do wrong. He gave His Son to die for our sins. Trust in Christ. Good works can't save you. Tarot cards, crystals, and positive energy can't save you, either. Only Jesus Christ can save you.

Next, strive to do the right thing even when it's not the popular thing. Bad situations can still produce good results. God truly does work in mysterious ways.

Finally, never lose your sense of humor. Life is tough, and you are going to need to learn how to laugh. If you don't, there's going to be plenty of tears.

From the bottom of my heart, thank you for taking time to read this book, or any other books I've written through the years. Whether I know you personally or have never met you, you made me a part of your life, and for that, I'll always be grateful.

God bless you all.

ADDITIONAL ACKNOWLEDGMENTS

This was perhaps my least favorite part of writing this book. While I believe you must give credit where credit is due, crediting all these sources brought back all the painful memories of book reports from my past and having to follow certain writing formats down to the letter or risk getting a lower letter grade. I'm very grateful to all the people who made these sources available, and I apologize if I didn't credit them in the right format. Some people cite their sources using the APA format whereas others use the MLA format. I got lazy and just went with the basic DSM format: "Don't Sue Me."

Anarchy TV Redux. "The Adventures of Pete and Pete Sick Day." YouTube. 7 August 2019. Web. 12 August 2019.

BUZZRPlus+, "Sale of the Century Episode #1 Jack/Andra/Buck." YouTube, 19 October, 2015. Web. 19 August 2019.

Joe Danziger. "Perfect Strangers – Baby Babka Ditty Song Scene." YouTube, 27 March 2017. Web. 12 August 2019.

runbuddyrunnow, "Perfect Strangers, Just Desserts, Bibbi Babka Go Boom." YouTube, 25 May 2014. Web. 12 August 2019.

Ryan S Geller, "Press Your Luck - The Whammies." YouTube, 25 January, 2011. Web. 12 August 2019.

The Student Bible, New International Version, With Notes by Philip Yancey and Tim Stafford, Zondervan Publishing House, Grand Rapids, Michigan, 1992.

Take Me To VHS Land, "(The All New) Let's Make A Deal - Game Show - 1985 - Monty Hall." YouTube, 30 September, 2017. Web. 7 October 2019.

Wikipedia contributors. "Autonomous sensory meridian response." *Wikipedia, The Free Encyclopedia*. Wikipedia, The Free Encyclopedia, June, 2019. Last edited 3 Aug. 2019. Monday 12 Aug. 2019.

Wikipedia contributors. "The Adventures of Pete & Pete." *Wikipedia, The Free Encyclopedia*. Wikipedia, The Free Encyclopedia, September, 2019. Last edited 17 September, 2019. Saturday 21 Sept. 2019.

Wikipedia contributors. "Perfect Strangers (TV Series)." *Wikipedia, The Free Encyclopedia*. Wikipedia, The Free

Encyclopedia. Last edited 8 Aug. 2019. Monday 19 Aug. 2019.

zorelis diaz, "Adventures of Pete and Pete, The S1E04 What We Did On Our Summer Vacation." YouTube, 3 April 2019. Web. 12 August 2019.

I would like to graciously thank the following YouTube ASMR, horror story, and exploration channels for providing me with the inspiration and information I needed to finish this book. Any YouTube related story ideas I featured in this book came from the content of these channels and *not* from the contents of my brain:

Ace's Adventures,
ASMR Darling,
Being Scared,
Blue Spooky,
CharlieBo313,
CrinckleLuvin ASMR,
Darkness Prevails,
Gentle Whispering ASMR,
Gibi ASMR,
Goodnight Moon,
Hellfreezer,
HorrorStudio1,
Killer Orange Cat,
Lets Read!,
Mr. Nightmare,

Ozley,
Prim ASMR,
The Proper People,
Retail Archaeology,
RnK All Day,
Seafoam Kitten's ASMR,
Soft ASMR,
SophieMichelle ASMR,
SouthernASMR Sounds,
Taylor ASMR,
This is Dan Bell.,
Unit #522,
VisualSounds1 ASMR,
The White Rabbit ASMR,
& WildKiss ASMR

P.S. I don't know if it's a good idea to watch *both* ASMR videos and horror videos right before going to bed, but if you do, there's a good chance you'll have some of the most relaxing nightmares you'll ever have in your entire life.

Printed in the United States
By Bookmasters